Patrick Cave

# All That Glitters

# All That Glitters

Lessons From My Life Searching For Gold

**Patrick Cavanaugh**

Mill City Press, Maitland

Mill City Press, Inc.
2301 Lucien Way #415
Maitland, FL 32751
407.339.4217
www.millcitypublishing.com

ISBN-13: 978-1-63505-067-7
LCCN: 2016914541

Cover Design by: Alan Pranke
Typeset by: Lydia Fusco

*Printed in the United States of America*

# CONTENTS

# INTRODUCTION

"There's gold, and it's haunting and haunting; It's luring me on as of old;
Yet it isn't the gold that I'm wanting, so much as just finding the gold . . ."
—*Robert Service*

If mankind's greed can be summed in a single word, that word might be—
gold! The word *gold* might also be used as a symbol of mankind's hope. Humans first discovered gold many thousands of years ago in streams all over
the world. It became an important part of every culture and continues to be
important today as an anchor of value for all nations. Through the eons many
people have spent lifetimes seeking gold. I am no different. During much of my
time on earth, I have worked as a gold exploration geologist. Some people may
say I am lucky to have reached my career objective and to have discovered two
large gold deposits. In today's prices, one of those gold deposits has a value in
excess of $840 million and the other (for which my company owns a royalty)
has a value in excess of $10 billion.

But my life is golden without the gold. My money and my possessions
are not what make me happy or fulfilled. As I reflect on my life, I realize that
my joy is proportional to what I have learned and how much I have loved. The
knowledge I have gained has been more valuable than gold.

My life began just three and one half months before the dawn of the
1950s. Therefore, my own decades of living correspond nicely to historical
decades. Within every ten-year time period, I have learned one lesson that has
been important to me. I want to share each lesson in this story of my life.

My own stories reveal how I learned each lesson. For centuries, many
other people, both ordinary and luminary, have learned and taught these same
lessons. My hope is that my readers might make some discoveries of their own

in my stories and that they will pass on their golden knowledge to others.

In a recent workshop I was asked, "If you were to sum up your role in life in one word, what would that word be? Husband? Father? Friend? Artist? Reader? Outdoorsman? Geologist? Adventurer? Traveler? Collector?" The answer is all of these descriptions are partly true, but none really cover all of what I am or what I have been. If I were to describe myself in a single word, that word would be *student*. My life's purpose has been to learn and to grow as a result of my learning. I continue living and learning as a student today, and I am writing this life story as a student sharing with other students.

Writing this autobiography has been an adventure of discovery. The act of thinking about my past has helped me to gain greater insight into my thoughts, my feelings, my strengths, and my weaknesses. I understand the roots of my own identity a little more because I have retraced some of the steps in my life's journey. I have discovered a greater appreciation for my friends, family, acquaintances, strangers, and even enemies who have contributed so much to my life. I also have discovered that most of the problems I have encountered and blamed on others were at least in part my own doing. I hope each reader will enjoy reading about the events that have shaped me. I also suggest that each of you consider writing about the lessons of your own lives. The process of self-reflection is valuable—just like nuggets of gold.

Make no mistake—I realize that God has blessed me in many ways. I was born in the greatest country on earth and I have had many opportunities others didn't have. I have felt God's presence throughout my life and He is the ultimate source of all my gold.

# <u>The 1950s:</u>
## Less Fear Results in More Freedom

"Ultimatelly we know deeply that the other side of every fear is a freedom."

*—Marilyn Ferguson*

# CHAPTER ONE: BEGINNINGS

I was born at about two a.m. on a Saturday morning on August 13, 1949, at the Deaconess Hospital in Bozeman, Montana. My mother and father lived in nearby Belgrade, Montana. In those days, Belgrade was a little farming town of 663 people, a place where our family knew everyone else and where everybody was like a family that helped each other to make ends meet. Small-town life in 1950s Montana was grand. We enjoyed our small-town sanctuary, our neighborly friendships, and our considerable liberty. If one morning someone's car didn't start, a neighbor helped him get it going. If a pump wasn't working, one of the neighbors helped fix it. People worked together without hesitation because they cared about their neighbors. Nobody locked his house or car because we didn't fear the other citizens of Belgrade.

During the first decade of my life, I was an innocent child protected from fears about the world. Most Americans in the 1950s were also like innocent children. We didn't yet have 24/7 television and Internet coverage of every news event worldwide, so we were effectively cloaked in a veil of innocence. We heard little about child predators, pornographers, or terrorists. Those bad people existed, but we really didn't realize that they could live nearby. Our innocence and naïveté enabled most of us to enjoy immense freedoms.

My first ten years were a magical time, a time I spent enveloped in the radiant love and optimism of my parents and other adults. In 1952, we moved from Belgrade to Billings, Montana. Although Billings was a larger town of about 31,000, it was still a very safe environment. Our small family had few fears and enjoyed boundless freedom. Billings was built along the Yellowstone River, the longest undammed river in the contiguous United States and one of the finest trout streams in the world. From Billings, we could drive to hundreds of nearby lakes, rivers, and mountains. Dirt roads granted access to almost every fathomable remote location for hunting, fishing, rock collecting, or berry picking, and our light green 1953 Ford climbed the mountains like a Jeep. The abundance of wild animals in Montana in the 1950s was staggering. Some evenings we would count hundreds of deer and antelope near the highway. It was not uncommon to see moose, elk, and other animals whenever we went out of town. Fish of many types swam in great abundance through the pristine lakes and streams of the region. Our Forest Service and Bureau of Land Management-administered lands remained accessible to the public and we never encountered designated trail maps or closed roads. Very few places were "off limits"; the whole world was ours to explore and enjoy.

In Billings, my childhood was simple and secure. When I was about five years old, my dad took my mother, my baby sister Mary, and me fishing on the Yellowstone River. We fished with worms gathered from our backyard that day. The sun was warm on my face and the river sparkled like a thousand jewels. I remember the smell of green grass, fresh air, and the river. As soon as my worm hit the water, the tug on the line was quick and strong. I pulled back and felt the pole bend all the way to the water as the trout ran with the bait. My joy was electric. While my parents watched, I hooked and landed my first big rainbow trout. The massive fish flopped and splashed all over me. Mom and Dad lovingly cheered my catch and offered considerable praise. Our dog, Duke, walked over, sniffed the fish, and wagged his tail in approval. That was the proudest moment in my five-year-old life. In my mind, I still can clearly see that big, beautiful rainbow trout shimmering in the sunlight. Every time I see a rainbow trout, I relive that wonderful feeling of pride and love.

Patrick Cavanaugh at age five with a rainbow trout from the Yellowstone River.

To enhance our family's fishing and hunting experiences and to save money, Dad decided to build a new boat in our basement in Billings. He found a design in one of his magazines—*Outdoor Life*, I think. He spent considerable time cutting all the wood precisely with a table saw and a coping saw, kicking up a layer of fine, pleasant-smelling sawdust. He sanded all the pieces, and then he began the process of steam heating the boards and slowly bending them into position. Wood screws were inserted to hold everything together.

After assembling the boat, my father had a surprise. It would not fit through the basement door! My mother delighted in retelling this tale throughout the years. Undeterred, Dad painstakingly took it apart and reassembled it outdoors. This time, he used both marine glue and wood screws to secure the joints. The rebuilt boat was deceptively well made. Dad added a substance, relatively new at the time, to the outside surface of the boat: fiberglass. The fiberglass made the boat much stronger and more resistant to punctures and abrasions. He painted the boat an ugly khaki color so that it would be camouflaged for hunting purposes. When it was all finished, he and I stood side by side on the lawn, silently admiring his craftsmanship.

Cavanaugh family in their homemade boat.

Left to Right—Patrick, Charles, Duke, Ken, and Mary.

Our family owned that boat for more than thirty years, and my father used it almost every weekend. Three times he added a new fiberglass coat. The boat did not fail us even in rough weather and big waves. Many wonderful fishing and hunting memories were made because of the confidence we had in that boat. It gave us the freedom to cruise so many Montana and Idaho lakes and rivers.

My younger sister Mary, younger brother Ken, and I were all born during the Baby Boom. In 1950, there were 47.3 million children under the age of eighteen living in America. By 1960, there were 64.5 million children under the age of eighteen. The Baby Boom was caused by the end of World War II and the dawn of a new era of American optimism about the future. Couples that had postponed getting married and starting a family during the war were now free to do both.

The 1950s were a boom time in another way. Buoyed by confidence in America's economic prospects, the entire economy burgeoned and the GNP went from $200 billion in 1945 to $500 billion in 1960. We felt this rising prosperity in our lives too. We moved from a tiny home in Belgrade to a larger new home in Billings. Then in 1956, we moved to an even larger new brick home in Idaho Falls, Idaho. My father started work as an electrician and electrical job planner for various contractors at the National Reactor Testing Station (NRTS), located in the desert about fifty miles outside Idaho Falls.

When my parents told me that we would be moving to Idaho Falls, I was afraid to leave my happy and secure life in Billings. In my mind I pictured Idaho Falls as a massive waterfall (like the Lower Yellowstone Falls) with a couple of log cabins at the base. As frequently happened in the 1950s, my unwarranted fears caused me to feel apprehensive when I should have felt great joy. I was so relieved when I saw Idaho Falls for the first time. In many ways, Idaho Falls was like Billings, only better. Idaho Falls was booming because the jobs at the NRTS paid nicely and the majority of the middle class families had extra money to spend.

When we arrived in Idaho Falls, our cab driver had never heard of Skyline Drive, which in 1956 was just a gravel road on the edge of town. Our house was one of only three or four on the street. Farm fields surrounded us in all directions, full of pheasants, doves, and other game animals. We enjoyed a great view of the Mormon temple along the Snake River and the more distant Teton Mountains from our living room window.

The author is ready for school at age eight. Our Idaho Falls home on Skyline Drive appears in the background. The 1953 Ford is in the garage.

During the 1950s my mother taught us that our fears could hurt other people. Politically, my mother was a liberal thinker and a strong supporter of FDR and the later presidential candidate, Adlai Stevenson. Mom had a heart for people who were less fortunate. She strongly supported the election of women, Blacks, and other minorities to any political office. She believed that everyone should have an equal opportunity in life and she made it clear to us kids that minorities did not have the same opportunities as we did.

Nevertheless, change was on the horizon. The 1950s was an important decade for the civil rights movement and the beginning of rights and opportunities for Blacks. This decade saw the first major victories for civil rights in the Supreme Court, the outbreak of nonviolent protests, and the evolution of Dr. Martin Luther King, Jr. into the movement's preeminent leader. My mother helped all of us children become keenly aware that life in the 1950s was very different for Blacks. We Caucasians in the majority feared people who were different, and our fears relegated people of color to second-class status and limited their freedoms and opportunities.

Despite the prosperity and optimism of the era, the 1950s were also marked by widespread fear of communism. These new fears would ultimately take away some other freedoms and, for an unfortunate few, would greatly change their lives. After WWII, the Russians had sought to control as much territory as possible, and Mao Zedong—more commonly known as Chairman Mao—had won the revolution in China. In the United States, people began to fear a global communist plot to conquer the world.

The "commies" thus became our common enemy. Senator McCarthy and his followers feared that some communist enemies were already secretly working in our country. Between 1945 and 1952, Congress held eighty-four hearings to put an end to "un-American activities." The mass hysteria over communism, enabled in part by people in the highest levels of government, caused tens of thousands of Americans in government, in universities, and in Hollywood to lose their jobs. These innocent people also lost their families and friends during the "Red Scare" of the 1950s.

These fears worsened when we entered the Korean War in 1953. Now the United States truly *was* at war with the communists. Meanwhile, in the idylls of Montana and Idaho, that war seemed a million miles away. Life for us was good and carefree and most of us did not worry about communists.

Once the Soviets had detonated an atomic bomb, we Americans began to fear a global atomic war. Atomic scientists who originally worked on the Manhattan Project constructed a doomsday clock in Chicago, for which certain events would move the hands on the clock one tick closer to midnight, the symbolic time at which the scientists predicted a nuclear war would wipe out the planet.

These scientists had real fears and they wanted the rest of America to be fearful too. A new Federal Civil Defense Administration (FCDA) was set up in 1951 to educate the country on how to survive an atomic attack from the Soviet Union. The FCDA commissioned a university study on how to achieve "emotion management" during the early days of the Cold War. One of their approaches was to involve schools. Teachers in selected cities were encouraged to conduct air raid drills in which they would suddenly yell "Drop!" and students were expected to kneel down under their desks with their hands clutched around their heads and necks to brace themselves for the nuclear onslaught (which thankfully never came). We participated in those duck and cover drills in my schools. Meanwhile, public fallout shelters were designated and survivalist -minded and fearful families built a few private shelters. Plans for shelters appeared in many magazine advertisements of the day. Although the possibility of global nuclear war was real, my father and mother thought the government and the survivalists were overly zealous and overly fearful. They doubted we were on the precipice of a nuclear calamity, and so our family decided not to waste time or money on a shelter.

As a boy, there were many times when my own fears were unrealistic. When I held on to those silly fears, some bad things happened to me. A painful memory from that decade was when I went to school with a bad earache. A cold Montana wind was blowing on that April day, and in the morning, my ear began to throb. We had to walk on fresh plywood boards to our new school so we didn't walk in the mud. My free hand covered my ear from the icy wind while my other hand carried my red and silver metal lunch pail. Every few minutes I would switch hands.

By the time I reached the school, my ear felt like it was on fire. My fears prevented me from telling the teacher that I had an earache all day long. By the late afternoon, I thought I would burst from the pain, but still I said nothing. I was relieved when the bell rang at the end of the day so I could go home and get some help for my sore ear. Overcoming my fear on that school day would have saved me from considerable pain.

During the first and second grade, I was sick so often with either an earache, sore throat, swollen glands, or fever that my parents and the doctors thought that I might have had rheumatic fever. However, a new doctor concluded tonsillitis was the cause of my recurrent ailments. He prescribed that I have my tonsils surgically removed.

Before the operation, I nervously tried to ready myself for surgery. The more I thought about the operation, the more my fears increased. As the day of the surgery approached, my anxiety ballooned to the point that I could think of nothing else.

Then, my mother took my brother and sister to the same doctor for an examination. The doctor advised that they, too, needed their tonsils removed. In fact, the doctor told us that nearly everyone should have their tonsils removed because tonsils were unnecessary. My mother reacted to that advice by taking my brother and sister home and cancelling my operation. I was very relieved, but it was a hollow feeling knowing I had spent all that time obsessing and worrying so much about an event that did not happen. Today my tonsils continue to be fine and form a part of my healthy immune system.

When I was about ten years old, I was selected to appear on a local television quiz show for kids in Idaho Falls. I don't remember the name of the show, but the host was a clown—actually a grown man dressed in a clown suit. I was very excited, and at the same time, my nerves were on maximum alert. My self-talk revealed my fears: "What if I make a fool of myself?" "What if I stumble and fall?" "What if I wet my pants?" My fears were my enemy because I could not control them.

On the day of the show, my fears made it difficult to think. My answers to the questions on the live television show were not consistent with my knowledge. Nevertheless, I won a spud gun (a metal gun that shot potato plugs) and some other small prizes like Idaho Spud candy bars. I knew I could have answered the questions so much better if I could have controlled my fears. My parents loved me and were proud of me no matter how I performed. Still today, I wish I could have conquered my fears and won a big prize.

When I was young, I feared eating new and different foods. My mother had been cooking for her family since she was five years old, and consequently, her dishes were spectacular. Often I turned down invitations to eat at my friends' houses because I was afraid I couldn't eat their food. I was such a finicky eater that I couldn't eat hamburgers from a drive-in restaurant or virtually anything at the school cafeteria. Many days I worried all morning about what we would have for lunch and whether I might be forced to eat. Eventually my food fears decreased and my taste buds changed. I regret the several years of my youth when I was handicapped by my fears and limited tastes.

At the end of the fourth grade, my class participated in a field trip. The class's collective excitement grew as the day approached. Our field trip was held in a big grass field on the edge of town and we played many different games. Adjacent to the field was a one hundred-year-old mansion with white columns, which was opened to the students. I had lots of fun playing games in the field all day and I soon needed the bathroom. I was too shy to ask my teacher for permission. Other students were getting permission, but I was too afraid. As the day continued, my urge to use the bathroom increased until it was all that I could think about. But still, my fear prevented me from saying anything.

Finally, I couldn't hold it any longer, and as the day ended, I wet my pants. The embarrassment of having all the kids in my class and my teacher see me with wet pants was visceral. All of this happened because of my fear to ask my teacher for permission to use the restroom!

Most of the time, my younger brother and sister and I were very shy and quiet, just like our mother. Most strangers complimented our mother and father on our behavior. They said things like "You have such good children" or "Your kids are so well behaved." In truth, we were just quiet and shy because we were afraid of strangers and new situations. My fears kept me in a kind of bondage. I was afraid to be my true self and often I stuffed my feelings instead of expressing them. Sometimes I was afraid to fully experience my life. Today I still struggle with my fear of new situations, but most of the time I can overcome my fear with love. When I realize I am becoming fearful, I remember the good in all of humanity and I choose to send out love to others. The act of loving others instantly lifts my fears and sends them away.

Sometimes I saw examples of the effects of fear in others. We had a new house in a new neighborhood in Billings. My father built an artistic cement and stone sidewalk in our backyard. It curved back and forth artfully in several directions and was adorned with beautiful multicolored rocks. The Rimrock cliffs along the Yellowstone River near Billings were composed of the Eagle Sandstone unit, and choice colored, flat rocks were easily available. Dad spent several days gathering rocks and hauling them to our home.

Our next-door neighbor admired my father's work and decided to build a stone and cement sidewalk of his own. When our neighbor ventured out to pick up his own rocks, he was startled by a large rattlesnake lying beneath one of the stones. He quickly decided to abandon that project, even though rattlesnakes were fairly uncommon in that area. His irrational fear of more snakes stopped him in his tracks, and as a result he was never able to enjoy his own rock sidewalk.

My mother contended with some fears, too. She grew up on a farm where transportation consisted of horses and a wagon in the summer or sleighs in the winter. There were no cars on her farm near Winifred, Montana. Throughout the 1950s in both Belgrade and Billings, Mom did not drive. When we first moved to Idaho Falls, Mom still did not drive. She was so afraid of driving that she didn't even want to start the learning process. Instead, she had to walk everywhere and carry her groceries by hand. It was difficult for her to get to the other side of town in Idaho Falls.

In many ways, we children were disadvantaged by her inability to drive. If we missed the bus, we had to walk or ride our bikes for many miles to get to school—even in the icy winter. Dad was at work at the NRTS site in the desert and he couldn't come home even in an emergency. If we were sick at school, there was no alternative for us. We would be stuck at school all day. My mother's fears limited her freedom as well as ours. In 1962 (just one year before I was able to drive), Mom finally overcame her fear and she obtained her driver's license. Now we all had much more freedom.

My father and mother both loved us all dearly. However, their respective ways of viewing the world differed greatly. Mom sorted by similarities. If you put three coins in front of her, she would first tell you how they were alike. Dad sorted by differences, and that quality helped him become a great engineer. He would first tell you how the coins were different from each other. Dad also might have had some fears about appearing incompetent, perhaps because his father had been overly judgmental.

Because he sorted by differences and because he was fearful that we would not learn to be competent, Dad developed a habit of criticizing and belittling each member of our family. He did not want to hurt us—he loved us. Nevertheless, his fears not only limited our freedom, they also inhibited our self-esteem. Despite our mother's love and praises, our father's unkind comments wore us down like water erodes a canyon. In response, Ken and I became more sensitive and defensive. We learned to fire back criticisms of our own as we also sorted the world by differences. Unfortunately, our critical tendencies have over time turned into unwanted habits.

At times, our family had perhaps too little fear or respect for danger. In the fifties, my favorite toys were an electric train, an Erector set, and a chemistry set. The chemistry set would never make it through a modern safety review. It contained many poisonous and explosive chemicals like copper sulfate and metallic potassium. Those chemicals were both fun and dangerous. I spent many pleasant hours performing my own experiments. I didn't burn anything down, blow anything up, or injure myself, but a number of close calls resulted in burned floors, charred countertops, and the release of all kinds of stinky and potentially harmful gases.

When I was seven years old, I was given a single shot .22-caliber rifle for my birthday. Obviously, the age of seven is much too young for a child to own a gun, but my father was very strict about us learning safe shooting habits. He believed that the key to our safety was that we have constant supervision with the rifle, that we learn all the rules to be safe, and that we practice those rules 100 percent of the time.

I shot my first rabbit when I was ten and my first deer when I was twelve. I was a hunter for my first thirty-five years of life. My father and brother are hunters still. Nobody in our family has been killed or wounded by firearms, but we do have some stories of near misses.

When I was a kid, the other half of our basement in Idaho Falls became a shooting gallery. Yes, a real shooting gallery. We stacked hundreds of old catalogues and magazines to make an impenetrable backstop. The catalogues and magazines did a fair job of catching the bullets from our .22-caliber rifles, although an occasional ricochet off the cement sent us ducking for cover.

There were many examples of my father's cavalier attitude toward safety in the outdoors. On one ice-fishing trip to Mud Lake, we transported five or six kids from our Idaho Falls neighborhood in addition to my brother and me. Our 1960 Ford station wagon was packed full with people and fishing gear as we drove out on the ice. It was a sunny spring day, about forty-five degrees, and melt water had ponded in many locations on the ice surface. A portion of the lake consisted of open water. I warned my father that the ice was thin, but he was determined to enjoy the ice fishing that day.

As we drove rapidly through the melt water on the ice, the water sprayed up on both sides. From the inside, it appeared that our station wagon had become a boat and the water was parting with our passage. The slushy ice was so soft and thin that all of us could feel the car sink down, straining dangerously under the weight of our Ford Ranch Wagon. Miraculously, we survived, and ending up catching a gunnysack full of perch. I don't believe anyone ever told the other kids' parents about the ice-flexing incident.

Another example of my father's lack of fear for thin ice occurred on a hunting trip when I was twelve. I strongly hoped to shoot a goose; it was the most difficult bird for a neophyte hunter to bag. We were hunting along the Snake River as it entered American Falls Reservoir. Ice lined the river and created a Venturi effect in which the water velocity was increased. The rushing water was very loud and sounded like a jet engine. When I saw the distant flock, my heart started pounding. I crouched down and then didn't move a muscle. As the flock passed, I raised my twenty-gauge shotgun and fired three times. The lead goose folded on my first shot and fell into the rushing river. My father was farther away and didn't have a shot, but he saw my first goose fall. I shouted with joy and then realized my happiness was premature. The goose was moving quickly along the river, and the ice prevented me from getting close enough to grab it. I chased the dead goose along the river until the river slowed as it entered the ice-covered reservoir. The goose was caught along the leading edge of the ice. Suddenly I realized that I was not going to get my goose.

My father saw what had happened and he started walking out from the other side to retrieve the goose. He immediately fell through the ice into the freezing water. He climbed out and found a stout stick. He banged on the ice with the stick to test the thickness before he proceeded forward. Eventually he made it to the ice edge and retrieved my goose by hooking it with the stick. I was happy to have the goose, but I felt a hollow feeling realizing that my father had risked his life to bring it home.

In Idaho Falls, we lived a free and peaceful life. My parents never locked our front door whether we were at home or away. They said, "If you ever have to lock your door, you need to move to a new house because you are living in the wrong place." During nice weather, the door would be open wide, with just an unlatched screen as protection from the insects and other unwanted guests. Sometimes we would sleep on the couch next to that unlocked door, free of any worry that someone would break in.

Summer was a time for backyard sleep-outs. On clear nights, we would stare at the stars, which seemed so close and bright that they were inviting us to touch them. There was less light pollution in my youth, and in the pitch-black sky, the stars glowed like millions of grains of sand on a moonlit beach. On other nights, lightning waltzed across the heavens, providing our entertainment until the rain forced us inside. Such were the days and nights of a childhood lived without worry. Our biggest concern was that our dogs would come out and lick our faces as we lay gazing at the stars.

Our parents saw the town as a friendly and peaceful place, so we had the freedom to walk or ride our bikes anywhere if we got permission. Frequently, we pedaled to nearby baseball fields and parks. If we had a few pennies in our pocket, we could go to Skyline Drug and order "Ironport" or "dashboard" soda in the five-cent, ten-cent, or fifteen-cent size. An Ironport was a regionally popular soda drink that combined root beer and Caribbean spices. A dashboard was a soda that blended all the different flavors, from orange to Coke. We would also ride or walk to the Skyline Lanes bowling alley and bowl a few lines. We rode to "birds' paradise," an abandoned, tree-covered farming area just outside of town, where we shot our BB guns at birds, ground squirrels, mice, and snakes to our hearts' content. We raised various vegetables and herbs in our garden and sold them to the nearby grocery store. Our family's dill was especially prized, and we were well compensated for it. Because we had no fear, the limits of our imagination were the only boundaries to our adventures.

Our parents also gave us the freedom to achieve difficult goals. Our resourcefulness was unhampered by a fear of failure. We were excited when the Coca-Cola Company ran a contest to collect their special edition bottle caps, which were printed with the fifty states on the bottom. Given our love of soda pop, this contest seemed like a godsend. The rules of the contest required a collection of bottle caps representing all fifty states glued on a collecting board. The prize for each completed board was a free six-pack of king-size Coke or Sprite, plus entry in a drawing for a ten-speed Schwinn bicycle.

Drinking enough Coke to collect all fifty different states would have been a huge task for any family. But my brother and I had an idea about how to outwit the contest makers. We knew that the pop bottle caps were magnetic, so we used electrical tape to attach a diminutive but strong alnico magnet to a straightened coat hanger: the perfect implement for fishing bottle caps out of the pop machines all over town.

We already had the freedom to ride our bikes to every bowling alley, every restaurant, and every business that had a Coke machine. With our pliable, magnetic instruments, we would fish out all the bottle caps through the cap-containing labyrinth in each machine. After a month, we filled fifteen to twenty huge garbage bags with bottle caps, which we then laid out on the lawn under the bright blue sky and sorted into piles for each state. Finally, in triumph, we would glue the caps in the appropriate location until the map was filled out.

Collectively, we turned in more than twenty-five complete boards. And my brother Ken won the ten-speed Schwinn bike! Yet, looking back today on the total sugar consumed, I wish we had not been so clever and tenacious.

For our family, the decade ended with a bang. On August 17, 1959, we had all gone to bed and had just started to sleep when at precisely 11:37 p.m., the walls began shaking. My mother and father heard the closet doors rattling, and when they got up, the floor was trembling. The sound of barking dogs interrupted the stillness of the night, and the people in our neighborhood went outside their homes and looked north toward the National Reactor Testing Station, fearing there had been an explosion there. But there was no mushroom cloud on the horizon, just the sound of barking dogs.

The next day we learned what had happened. A 7.5-magnitude earthquake had struck near Hebgen Lake, Montana, about seventy-five miles from Idaho Falls. It was felt in nine western states and three Canadian provinces. It was one of the strongest earthquakes in North America, comparable in magnitude to the devastating 1906 San Francisco earthquake. The quake tilted Hebgen Lake and caused large waves to pass over the dam. The Hebgen Lake dam did not break, but the quake caused severe devastation in other areas. A landslide plummeted down on twenty-eight campers in the Madison River Valley and buried them alive. More than 50 million cubic yards of earth slid down the mountain, across the valley, and partly up the other side. But as nature destroys, so does it create: a new lake—Quake Lake—was born, and new geysers and cracks developed in nearby Yellowstone National Park.

Nevertheless, after the earthquake, we acted just as we had before. We continued to go camping and fishing. We frequently went to Hebgen Lake, Quake Lake, and the Madison River. We did not let our fear of another quake limit our freedom.

I am grateful for many people in my life during the 1950s and beyond. Each shared their gifts with me, and I owe them much. Throughout my life my mother was as good as any mother could be. She showed her love every day in a thousand ways and cared for all my needs. She was not only a loving mother, she took on added roles of room mother, Cub Scout den mother, gourmet chef, PTA vice president, and school crossing guard. She devoted her life to her family, and she was happy doing just that.

My father taught me to love the outdoors, to fish, to hunt, to ice skate, and to play baseball. He was a renaissance man who could not only repair almost anything, but fabricate all the parts from objects just lying around the garage (for example, he made a crossbow from an automobile leaf spring and old gunstock). Most of all, he was a good friend to me—and he still is at age ninety-six.

My sister was a serene person who cared greatly about other people, especially her children. She almost always put the needs of others ahead of her own. She was an artist—she loved making and viewing art. She had a difficult life but rarely complained. She died in a tragic accident in a shopping mall. She taught me to laugh at life's challenges.

My brother was, and continues to be, a good friend, a gentleman, and a first-class human. He has loved and supported me throughout my life. His zest for the outdoors is exemplified by the long hours he spends fishing, hunting, golfing, and hang gliding. Together we have made, and continue to make, memories.

I didn't meet my half-sister, Betty, until after I graduated from high school. Betty was the daughter of my father and his first wife, Elizabeth Adams. My dad and Elizabeth were married at a young age just before my father headed off to WWII. Their marriage didn't last but fortunately our family renewed ties with Betty in later years. Although I have only spent a few days with Betty in every three or four years, I feel I know her well and I truly love her. She has impressed me greatly with her love, persistence, patience, and self-sacrifice. Betty has been a sweet wife, a loving mother, and a giving grandmother. She is a wonderful example to everyone in our family.

In my youth I learned about fear. I learned that everyone feels fear. It is a natural emotion and it often protects us from danger. I learned that once I conquered my fears, my freedom expanded in many ways. I learned that holding onto unrealistic fears could injure both myself and others. Finally, I learned that fear is such a powerful emotion that sometimes it can only be conquered by love. Today I am still learning how to conquer my fears, broaden my freedom, and inflict less harm on other people.

Fear is one of mankind's most basic and innate emotions. It is a necessary response to physical and emotional danger. Some fears are evolutionary adaptations that have been useful in the past. For example, the fear of heights might have developed in all mammals during Mesozoic time. The fear of snakes may have arisen during the Cenozoic time period and may be common to all simians. The fear of mice and insects might be unique to humans and may have developed much more recently during the Paleolithic and Neolithic eras. However, while at some point these fears served a distinct evolutionary purpose, today they are often disproportionate to the actual threat (for example, the fear of snakes). Our fears are not valid when we misinterpret either the risk or the seriousness of the threat. Unjustified or irrational fears can be our enemy and inflict unnecessary pain and suffering on others and ourselves. When we reduce our fears, our freedoms grow.

Life then was a joyous experience. The love I felt from my parents, my brother and sister, and my friends helped me to overcome my fears and to enjoy a blissful childhood. When I reflect on those memories, I feel the love radiate within me, and I smile. It was a time of learning, exploration, and growth. I learned in particular the thing that would stay with me my whole life, the lesson that would come to influence everything I did, and do: the other side of fear is freedom. Living with little fear in the wide-open spaces of Montana and Idaho was a great preparation for the next decade: the turbulent 1960s.

# The 1960s:

## Friends Are Worth More than Gold

"A friend is a treasure more precious than gold,
For love shared is priceless and never grows old."

*—Anonymous*

# CHAPTER TWO: A STABLE AND STATIONARY HOME BASE

During the 1960s, my family remained on Skyline Drive in Idaho Falls. My stable and stationary home base made it much easier for me to build a number of good friendships. Friends were my priority, and I had time to devote to being a friend. Many of my Idaho Falls friends remained close from second grade through high school and even into my early college years.

Like all kids, my first friends were also my playmates. As I grew older, I began to do everything with my friends and I spent most of my day with them. Later, I worked with many of these same friends. My elementary school friends were mostly boys, but in both junior high school and senior high school, I started to take an interest in girls, and some of them became my friends too. In high school, I met my first real girlfriend, and she continued to be my only girlfriend until I left for college. In college, I lived with many fraternity brothers as friends, and in my second year of college, I met a new type of girlfriend: the lady who would become my best friend, my lover, and my future wife.

The 1960s were a fascinating decade of massive social change, representing all that was revolutionary, subversive, and radical about the twentieth century. When John F. Kennedy took office in 1960, my family, like many families from coast to coast, believed that this handsome young president represented a spirit of hope for our nation. We were optimistic that he had the talent and energy to solve our many problems. Just two years later during the Cuban Missile Crisis, our country suddenly found itself on the brink of nuclear war with the Soviet Union. Later, Kennedy was assassinated and the Vietnam War began. Then the draft was instituted and young people were forced to fight a war that they did not support (and eventually one that the majority of US citizens did not support). The youth of the United States began to question the middle class values of their parents and started to believe that protests and disobedience were the means through which to express their dissatisfaction. Economic stability and birth control gave rise to new freedoms, and many young people became "hippies" and "flower children," clad in bell-bottom pants, miniskirts, and paisley shirts. Young people also rebelled by letting their hair grow and listening to radically different music than their parents. For the first time in the history of this country, there was a clear social rift between parents and their teen and young adult children.

The saying today among people my age is, "If you remember the sixties, then you weren't there," implying that if you weren't drunk, stoned on marijuana, or taking hallucinogenic drugs, then you didn't fully participate in that decade. Because I lived in a small, Mormon-dominated, Idaho town through high school, I was sheltered from much of the social change of the era. For most residents of Idaho Falls, the 1960s seemed to be happening somewhere else. Nevertheless, television greatly influenced our worldviews. Along with the whole country, our family watched with rapt attention as the assassinations of our president, his brother, and Martin Luther King, Jr. were played and replayed on television. We watched as President Johnson declined to run for reelection. We watched as the Tet Offensive made the Vietnam War look unwinnable. We watched as the United States triumphed in the race to the moon with the Russians.

The legacy of the sixties reverberates even today, and the events of the era evoke strong memories for those who lived through them. All of these events I experienced at a distance on television. It wasn't until I reached college that I began to really appreciate the "feelin' groovy" pulse of that era and to experience firsthand the growing freedoms of my youth.

When the decade began, I was ten years old and a student in the fifth grade, and when it ended, I was twenty and soon to be a married man. The 1960s was the decade of greatest change in my life, mimicking the massive change that swept the culture of the United States. It was essential for me to have many friends during my own period of growth, change, freedom, and experimentation. My friends amplified my joy, expanded my interests, helped me resolve my challenges, and assisted me with understanding my emotions during these formative years. With my friends, I learned how to play sports, how to work hard, and how to be more creative.

At the beginning of the decade, while in elementary school, I misunderstood one aspect of friendship. During fifth and sixth grades, I believed it was critical to be perceived as tough. The grade school hierarchy for boys was established by fighting. The tougher you were perceived to be, the higher your status. If you were weak, you were at the bottom. This presented a problem: I was smaller and weaker than the bigger boys.

Because of my small size, I thought others would consider me worthless and that they would tease me and pick on me. However, my two best friends in elementary school were reputed to be the two toughest boys in school (although nobody ever challenged them). Nobody ever picked on me and everyone was nice because they feared my friends. Looking back on this later, I learned that often we are controlled by our beliefs. I believed I was weak and thought I needed friends that others believed were strong. In truth, all I needed was to have more confidence in myself. As I grew older, I gained confidence in my abilities and my friends helped me feel better about myself.

Often, my father was my best friend. We shared many experiences and interests. In 1962, Dad and I went on an unforgettable adventure. We owned an old fifteen-horsepower Tote Goat motorcycle that had fat tires and low gearing. Together we drove the Tote Goat up the Middle Fork of the Salmon River and about ten miles into the Idaho Primitive Area. We went as far on the Tote Goat as the Forest Service rules allowed, and from that point we walked up Loon Creek to a series of pristine, untouched waterfalls.

We were all alone in the Primitive Area—there was no sign of other humans. We camped on the ground next to Loon Creek. He laid some pine branches on the ground to make both of our beds a little softer. I used an old sleeping bag and my father had only an army blanket as a cover. In the morning, our fire warmed us and so did our coffee.

We fished in the deep holes below the falls for wild Chinook salmon. The fishing was fantastic! There were so many rainbow and cutthroat trout in each hole that we always had an immediate bite on our salmon roe. After catching most of the trout in the hole, it was finally possible to get the salmon to bite. Dad said, "Just keep the salmon out of the falls or they will break your line and be gone." I managed to land my first salmon because I hooked it in a deep pool just beyond a nice landing beach. My second salmon quickly went into a waterfall and I lost it. Dad was right—my line broke. Both fish caused my heart and young mind to race. The trip was memorable for a thirteen-year-old boy because it was one of many times of bonding with Dad. With my father, I learned to appreciate the outdoors.

At age thirteen I caught my first Chinook salmon.

When Dad and I went hunting, we stayed in our 1958 Cardinal camping trailer. It was a much more luxurious way to camp and worked very well for hunting and other family camping activities because we slept on comfortable beds, stayed warm inside with furnace heat, and cooked on a propane stove and oven. Dad was quite a character and it was always an adventure to hunt with him. He was extremely knowledgeable about the art of hunting. He was fun to be with because he loved the outdoors so much and he had his own way of doing things. He also could string together long series of four letter words when things didn't work the way he anticipated.

It was November and there was snow on the ground, but Dad built a fire to keep us warm. He thought the bigger the better when it came to fires, and his was one of the biggest. He stacked wood and sagebrush to my height, and then he poured on a half-gallon of white gas. When he lit a match and threw it on the woodpile, the immediate conflagration roared to a height of fifty feet. I feared he would set the woods afire, but the flames quickly died to a manageable level and the presence of snow and moisture-laden trees prevented the disaster.

During the trip Dad decided to cook some greasy chicken in the oven. So seldom did my father cook that I feared the resultant meal. Usually nobody in the family could keep from gagging on the food he fixed. So I watched the chicken preparation with considerable apprehension. Dad had placed the chicken on a cookie sheet, and as the chicken cooked it produced a large amount of grease. The grease rose almost to the top of the sides of the cookie sheet, and my father thought it would be time to take the chicken out of the oven. He speared out the chicken with a fork and put the pieces on a plate on the table. Because the oven was still super hot, Dad decided to get the greasy cookie sheet out before it burst into flames. In place of potholders, my dad used a couple of paper towels. The paper towels proved to be woefully inadequate, and Dad's fingers began to feel the heat.

I am not sure exactly what went through my father's mind during the next few seconds. His face turned red and he started to yell from the pain on his fingers. Instead of heading for the table with the hot, grease-filled cookie sheet, he ran for the door. Unfortunately, I could see that the cookie sheet was slightly wider than the door. He hit the doorway going full speed, the sheet predictably flipped, and the super hot grease went all over my father's pants and the floor. The next forty seconds were filled with almost all the swear words in my father's vocabulary. I had tears in my eyes, but I bit my lip to keep from laughing. Dad and I cleaned up the mess together, and the next day we both laughed about the incident.

My friends and I enjoyed playing various team sports. We loved baseball, basketball, and football and would play at the parks, school fields, in our
back yards, and in our driveways. We would play all summer, after school, and
on weekends, regardless of the weather. Many times we played in the hot sun
and we "washed down" with a hose over our heads to cool off. It also helped
to drench our hats in water to stay cool. A few times we were soaked in the
rain before we could get home from the game, and a few games ended in a
snowstorm. Playing together helped us cement our friendships. The sporting
activities also helped to keep me fit throughout my life and, more importantly,
instilled confidence that I could keep up with the other boys and compete in
any area of my life.

The author wearing a little league uniform at age twelve.

My friends and I also engaged in outdoor sports in the winter. Occasionally, my
father put on his old skates. He was a very talented figure skater who could do
the splits on ice and make a perfect figure eight. When my sister Mary was four
or five years old, she received a pair of ice skates for Christmas. All that winter
she skated round and round the ice pond my father created in our back yard.

Gradually, her skating improved, and the act of watching her glide gracefully and rapidly across the smooth ice each day made me want to begin skating too. I was thrilled to get skates for Christmas the following year. Ice-skating transformed my wintertime life from one based on sitting indoors and reading books to a life that revolved around outdoor fun. Most winters I skated every day—and usually almost all day. My skills developed rapidly, and soon I was able to skate very fast and stop on a dime, covering anyone near me in a chilly spray of ice shavings. I could also skate backwards using the crossover leg motion of a hockey player or figure skater.

My friends and I would often play a game of tag on the ice, or we enjoyed informal hockey with brooms and cans or ice chips for pucks. Sometimes we would stack up sleds on the ice and jump over them. Once I caught my skate on the top of a sled in the middle of a jump, landed on my knee, and had a colorful knee the size of a small pumpkin the rest of the winter.

Many years we made a pond in our backyard. Later, the city of Idaho Falls created two larger skating ponds just a couple blocks from my house. There we skated until dinner, and then we went back again after dinner to skate on weekdays and weekends. Usually I would just grab my skates and go and my friends would show up at the ice ponds.

It is every child's dream to have a prime sledding hill, and we were lucky to have one just two blocks up Skyline Drive. It was a nice, long hill, and when the conditions were right and the snow was packed down well, it made for some rapid sledding. We used mostly wooden sleds with steel runners because they were fast and easy to steer. We sometimes would douse the hill with water at night so there would be a layer of ice to increase our speed. Sledding with my friends was so much fun that sometimes I couldn't tear myself away from it all and I returned home with minor frostbite on my fingers and toes. Later, we tied sleds behind a car with a rope and pulled them on deserted roads outside of town. It worked great unless we hit a bare spot in the road. Of course, these moments were made all the better because I shared them with my friends.

Every year around Christmas, I begged for skis, and every year I was disappointed. My parents thought that skiing was too dangerous and too expensive. Almost all of my high school friends were good skiers by the time I finally got my first pair of skis for Christmas in the eleventh grade. My third time skiing, I was at the Kelly Canyon Resort. I was a mere novice, but I could make a snowplow turn and an occasional stem christie. On my second run down the mountain, I was going faster than my abilities allowed. I planned to make a quick turn to slow my speed, but another skier turned right in my way. Now I was careening downhill about twice as fast as I had ever dared. As the hill steepened, trees flew in an evergreen blur on both sides, and I was totally out of control.

Suddenly, I caught the edge on my left ski and tumbled head over heels in a spectacular fall. Powdered snow flew up in a big cloud. Other skiers came over and formed a ring around me. It took a while before I even moved. They asked me if I was okay. I said, "I think so," but when I looked down, my left ski was broken completely in half! Thank goodness it wasn't my leg! Before I progressed to the intermediate stage as a skier, I broke two pairs of skis but luckily no bones.

My friends and I learned to be inventive in our outdoor play. We decided that the canal would be perfect for pulling water skiers because there was a two-wheel dirt track adjacent to the canal for miles. So we tied a rope to the car, obtained an old pair of water skis, and suddenly we were skiing. Getting pulled up on the skis was easy because the car would snap us up out of the water quickly. The rope pulled constantly to one side, so the skier had to apply pressure to the ski on that side. The fun stopped abruptly when the skier hit the canal bank. My friends and I also pulled each other on skis behind the car on snow-covered roads on the outskirts of town. We knew this activity was dangerous, and people did fall when they hit bare sections of roadway. The bare roads were also very hard on the bottoms of our skis.

My neighborhood friends and I were sometimes getting ourselves into trouble. Our favorite nighttime game in the summer was to play "raiders," a name inspired by our once-in-a-blue-moon practice of raiding the neighbors' gardens for tasty vegetables. Most of the time, we "raiders" just played a game of hide and seek and chase. We were skilled at jumping fences from yard to yard. The fences varied in height and type, and we learned how to leap over them quickly. We would wear black clothing so that we could hide more effectively, and we hid in the basement window wells or behind bushes. Any dark place was good. We could play outside until our parents called us, usually around ten p.m. in my case.

A few times our nighttime raiders play became more delinquent. We learned how to make time-delayed fuses from a particular type of string and could measure out just the right length for a fifteen-minute, a thirty-minute, or a one-hour delay. We tied these fuses to firecrackers or M-80s and left them on a porch or in a mailbox while we waited safely at home with our families when they exploded, obliterating their containers in a loud, fiery burst. We were never caught. Fortunately, our playful shenanigans caused only one or two instances of minor property damage, and nobody was ever injured.

My friends and I enjoyed many creative but questionable adventures interacting with mammals, fish, birds, reptiles, and amphibians. We rode our bikes to ponds near the Snake River and caught tadpoles with wire French fry cookers. We kept the tadpoles in a huge washbasin in our backyard. In a few weeks, they all turned into toads. Now we had more than 250 toads hopping throughout the backyard. Mom was not happy about the Biblical quantity of toads, and after a few days, we took them back to the river to release them.

We also caught baby magpies from nests in the cottonwood trees and raised them in pens we made at home. Our hope was to teach the magpies to talk like one of the neighbor kids had done. My magpie didn't live long enough to do so. A neighbor boy cared for our pets while we were on vacation. He accidently fed dog food to my magpie and that was the end of that project.

Sometimes my friends and I flirted with disaster. About a half-dozen times, we waded out in the Snake River below Idaho Falls. In the fast current at the base of the falls, we could catch one- to three-pound mudsuckers with our bare hands. The big fish would be pinned in the rocks by the force of the water and we learned how to feel them and then grab them. The resonance of the falls made it hard to hear, so we shouted to each other. I still remember the fishy smell of the Snake River, the ice-cold spray, and the roar. Even in the shallow water, the force was so great we were nearly swept off our feet. We would sometimes put a few of the suckers in the swimming pools of the nearby motels as a prank. Needless to say, our parents were oblivious to our activities, and we were very fortunate to avoid any injuries or drownings.

In high school, my friends and I took hunting trips together. We hunted deer and various game birds after school and on weekends. On one deer hunt, we took my friend Scott's 1952 Chevy and we shot two buck deer. Although my buck was smaller, it was a legal two-point and I was quite proud. We loaded my deer in the trunk, and Scott's larger four-point buck fit in the back seat. The front legs were hanging out one side and the head and antlers were hanging out the other side of the car. There were four of us on the hunting trip, so a friend and I had to ride in the back seat on top of the deer. We were so proud of our success that we wanted to blatantly show off the deer. We must have been quite a sight for other Frostop Drive-In patrons when we pulled in to place an order.

On a separate guys' trip, I took my father's Nissan Patrol into Wolverine Canyon near Taylor Mountain. The hike was short but steep up to 40 Horse Cave. It was rumored that the cave was so called because in the past, "rustlers" had used it as a place to hide their horses.

On our way to the cave, we heard a nearby cougar scream. A cougar scream sounds a lot like a woman screaming; it is a piercing scream that makes every cell in your body come alive in full alert. Nobody admitted they were scared, though we all were. Although we didn't know which animals might share the placid cave with us in the night, I finally drifted off to sleep.

About two a.m., my friend Steve thought he saw something in the opening of the cave and he pulled out his .45-caliber pistol. There can be few sounds louder than a .45-caliber pistol shot inside a cave in the middle of the night. The boom was so loud I thought my head would explode. After we regained our hearing and flashed our lights around the cave, we all yelled at our foolish friend for his stupidity. The rest of the night we didn't sleep. That was our only overnight trip to 40 Horse Cave.

On another trip, my father and I were hunting ducks and geese at the

Market Lake Wildlife Management Area near Roberts, Idaho, with my father's best hunting friend. We had been hunting at various locations on the frozen lake and sloughs. There was a nice supply of ducks using the few open water areas. In the afternoon, I was walking in an area away from the other adults. Although the ice was not thick, I wasn't concerned because I was wearing hip waders and most of the area we were hunting was shallow. If I fell through the ice, it was unlikely the water would go over my waders.

Sure enough, suddenly the ice gave way beneath my feet. Unfortunately, at that moment I happened to be in the middle of the lake in a deep spot. With a whoosh, I was suddenly plunged into the ice water. There was no time for fear, and I instinctively thrust my arms straight up and held my shotgun over my head. It was the horizontally held shotgun that caught on the ice and stopped my descent to the bottom of the lake.

Quickly, my waders filled with the ice water, making them heavy. The cold temperature took my breath away and I didn't want to remain there long; I held my gun flat on the edge of the unbroken ice and slowly lifted myself up. I broke the thin ice until the ice felt sufficiently solid to hold my weight. Then I was able to use my horizontally held gun to lift and roll myself back out on top. My lack of fear enabled me to make the correct choices to save my own life.

Frozen but exhilarated to be alive, I began walking towards our car and called for help. My father came running and then started the car and put the heater on. I emptied my boots and took off my wet clothing, wrapping a thick wool blanket around my shivering body. The trip home only took about twenty-five minutes, and I was soon able to get warm and tell my story to the rest of the family.

Sometimes my friends influenced my behavior positively. My neighborhood friend Bruce and I started a lawn mowing business together when I was twelve years old. We had six clients whose lawns we mowed weekly. We also caught the grass clippings and dumped them behind my house. Some of our clients were very particular about cutting length and other factors. One required us to cut with his rotary lawn mower, which he insisted was superior to our motorized reel-type mowers.

We enjoyed the work and the money. I used some of my earnings to customize my mower and I installed a straight exhaust pipe to make it louder and theoretically more powerful. Bruce and I worked together in our business for two summers until we both graduated to farm work. In my lawn business, I learned how to get along with a partner. I also learned that the customer is always right. These lessons would serve me well later in life.

While working with my friends, I acquired some other life lessons. Most importantly, I learned that many people have to work very hard for us to have the life we live. During our last year in junior high school and throughout high school, my friends and I worked together during the summers. None of us could get jobs in town, so we did farm work. Without my friends, I never would have labored so hard on farms for so many summers. Friends made the arduous farm work much more enjoyable.

We worked for several farmers near Idaho Falls, mainly moving irrigation pipe. We disconnected each forty-feet-long section of six-inch-diameter aluminum pipe, emptied the water by tilting the pipe to one side, carried the pipe about forty feet across the rows in the field, and then locked the section into the new row of pipe. With practice, we learned to balance and carry the heavy pipe on our thighs as much as possible to save stress on our backs. One pipe section could weigh up to ninety pounds when filled with water and mud.

For this work, we were paid $1.50 for moving the thirty-three sections of pipe in a quarter mile-long "line" covering the length of a field. Most of the time we moved a line in about an hour. If the mud was deep and the pipes were full, it took us an hour and a half or two hours per line. Once the line was moved, we turned on the water and checked to make sure that there were no blowouts or places where the pipe wasn't quite connected or where the risers had been blown off by the water pressure.

Our pipe-moving outfits consisted of sweatshirts, old shirts, old Levi jeans, and tall, waterproof rubber shoes. Usually the hauling and dragging and pulling and connecting left us soaked in water and mud from the waist down. I realize now that my mother must have had a good deal of laundry to do during those pipe-moving summers. We moved pipe in the early morning beginning about five a.m. and at night beginning about five p.m., since the pipe had to be moved every twelve hours. We might not get home from moving until ten p.m., or later if there were problems.

My brother Ken owned the best pipe-moving vehicle, a 1954 Hudson Super Wasp with a 262 cubic inch (4.3 liter) L-Head six engine fed by a two-barrel carburetor. My brother purchased "The Beast" for seven dollars at an auction held by the Idaho Falls Police Department. The engine was frozen when we tried to start the car, but we towed it down our alley and put it in gear. As soon as the clutch was popped, the engine fired, belching a considerable cloud of white smoke from the exhaust. Afterward, The Beast purred like a kitten. The Super Wasp was heavy, and when those big tires started turning, it moved through the mud like a great ship. Several times when there were blowouts in the irrigation system, we got various vehicles and farm equipment stuck. But the big Hudson was very dependable and it would always get us to work and home again.

The second lesson I learned was that sometimes farm work can be dangerous and safety is imperative. One day when I was pipe moving alone, a thunderstorm advanced closer and closer. The sky darkened and the wind picked up, but I chose to keep working. Suddenly a lightning bolt struck in the field and a big ball of blue fire rolled across the ground, burning some of the potato plants. The instantaneous thunder was deafening. I quickly dropped the aluminum pipe I was holding and lay down on the ground in a dry spot away from the pipe until the storm passed. Aluminum conducts electricity nicely, and a quarter-mile length of conductive pipe is a target for lightning.

The next lesson I learned was that some jobs can be more profitable and more enjoyable than others. During the middle of the day, we often hoed beets or hauled hay. We were paid three cents for "bucking," or lifting the hay up from the field and onto a trailer, and then three cents more for unloading the hay bales from the trailer onto the haystack. If we worked quickly, we could make from $1.50 to $3.00 per hour bucking and hauling hay. The task of hoeing beets was paid by the acre, and we usually worked with Mexican laborers. I liked hoeing beets the most because, by working quickly, I could earn even more money. A good beet hoer could make $4.00 to $5.00 an hour. The Mexicans taught me how to file my hoe to keep it sharp and to use a minimum of strokes to accomplish a maximum of work. I also learned all the swear words in Spanish—there were side benefits to our hard work.

Working on the farms with my friends was usually agreeable. However, farm work was sometimes exhausting. One year at the beginning of the season, my friend Bob and I were working on the haystack for a new farmer, unloading bales from trucks and trailers as they pulled up. As the work dragged on, we became covered from head to toe with a mixture of perspiration and hay dust. I sneezed continually and my eyes itched and watered something fierce. (This event alone might have been the beginning of my seasonal hay fever.) Because we were trying to impress our new boss, we exerted ourselves as much as physically possible that day, so much so that by the end of the day, we could barely stand or move.

When it came time to go, we climbed into Bob's Volkswagen Bug and we started to drive home. We soon realized we were too tired to even walk out of the car and into our houses, so we drove to a nearby park. Both of us rolled out of the Volkswagen and we lay on the grass for about an hour. We watched the clouds blow across the sky and we heard the birds singing in the trees. Gradually our energy flowed back into our bodies. Only then were we revived sufficiently to drive home and stagger into our respective houses.

My three years in high school were the best three years of my life, mainly because of my friends. It was a time in which I could feel unquenchable energy and joy in my blood. I was invigorated to go to school because I knew the day would be so enjoyable. High school was a time of not only enjoying the present, but anticipating a wonderful future.

My friends and I were not the most popular kids in school, but all of us were so very happy during our high school years because we had inner peace and we had each other as friends. The knowledge that my friends would support me when I needed them deeply enriched my time in high school. All of my high school friends were members of the Church of Jesus Christ of Latter Day Saints (Mormons). A group of Mormon girls went to parties and dances, played tennis, went skiing, and went snowmobiling with us. None of us were really boyfriends and girlfriends, but we did group activities together. My high school friends and I were always joking around and playing pranks—mostly on each other. We all had a great sense of humor and we enjoyed every minute we were together. Life was fun every day.

High school buddies at thirty-year, post-graduation anniversary golf tournament in Idaho Falls. Left to right: Mike, Patrick Cavanaugh (the author), Scott, and Heber.

On a warm May day, my friend Bob and I were cruising in his car near Tautphaus Park in Idaho Falls. We had filled twenty to thirty water balloons and we were searching for targets. Suddenly the perfect opportunity appeared. A Volkswagen convertible containing four cheerleaders from our high school was sailing down the road in the opposite direction. If I could time my throw correctly, we would get a direct hit on the cheerleaders. Because I was riding shotgun on the passenger side, I had to reach out and fling the water balloon up high over our car and into the other lane. In my enthusiasm to get the cheerleaders, I sent the balloon much too high into the air. The balloon came down a few seconds late on a big, ugly, Hells Angel-type motorcyclist who was driving in the same direction about one hundred feet behind the cheerleaders.

The balloon scored a direct hit and Mr. Hells Angel was soaked, and pissed. We looked in the mirror and saw that he had turned his motorcycle around and was in hot pursuit of us. Our adrenaline was instantly maxed and Bob floored his car. We were really flying, but the motorcycle was still gaining on us. We traveled for about three miles, making sharp turns left and right, with the biker hot on our trail. When we stopped for a traffic light, he pulled behind us and threw down his motorcycle. Up close he was even bigger and meaner than we first thought. He sported a mustache, a dark tattooed body, and an angry scowl. We were terrified when he grabbed Bob's door and opened it. Bob fought to close the door, and at the same time he accelerated the car forward because the light had turned green. As our car lurched ahead, the biker let go of the door and jumped back on his bike. This time we had enough of a lead that we were able to get to some high speed back roads and lose the biker. When we knew he was gone, Bob and I took the back roads home and hoped we would never see the biker again. We laughed when we shared the experience with our other friends the next day.

My high school buddies and I all looked forward to seeing each other in school, after school, and on weekends. We planned all sorts of activities together and we were usually inseparable. Our friendships were solid because we learned to put each other first.

Throughout my teens, my father often liked to tease me by saying that he would some day tell my first girlfriend about whatever embarrassing behavior I was doing at that moment. If I made a mess, picked my nose, or flubbed up some task, he would remind me that eventually he would get a chuckle from recounting it to her. His threats to tell my hypothetical girlfriend were repeated for years. My father so intimidated me that I was very secretive about any girls for fear that he would in fact tell them about all my embarrassments.

When I was a junior in high school, I started to notice one of the girls in my trigonometry class. Her name was Beverly (or Bev). I often flirted with her and she reciprocated. We became close friends and we learned that our fathers worked together at the NRTS site; in fact, Beverly's father was my father's boss. Bev was both pretty and smart and I had a crush on her.

One day, Beverly invited me to Idaho Falls High School's "girls' choice" Sadie Hawkins Day formal dance. To be honest, I was thrilled. I doubt that I ever would have been confident enough to invite her to a formal dance without her making the first move. My friends noticed my exuberant excitement about the upcoming date. I told my parents that I was going to the dance but didn't tell them whom my date was.

I rented a white dinner jacket and purchased a corsage, and I made reservations for dinner at a nice restaurant before the dance. When the evening finally arrived, Bev was a vision in her stunning yellow dress. We danced fast dances to most of the songs of the sixties, and when the music changed and it was time to dance slowly, we pressed ourselves close together and moved in slow, swaying rhythm to the gentle music. I think we both were somewhat smitten that night.

The next day, my father groused to his coworkers that his son had spent too much money on dinner, the formal rental, and the corsage. His boss said, "But he looked great." My father came home and said, "Why didn't you tell us that you were dating my boss's daughter?" I replied, "Because you were always teasing me about what you would tell my girlfriend." My mother laughed and said to my father, "Serves you right! Now quit teasing him."

The old saying that you remember your first love forever is also true for me. Beverly was my best friend, my girlfriend, and the one person I thought about all the time. She was impeccably kind, and an absolute knockout when she wore a bikini. She was not a Mormon, but she fit into my group of friends very well. We skied, skated, played tennis, and went to parties together as a group. Bev was quite athletic and loads of fun. She frequently asked how each of my friends was doing and she genuinely cared about everyone.

One Saturday, Bob and I invited our girlfriends to his house. Our girlfriends liked our calamari appetizers and the barbequed steaks for the main course. The girls were very flirtatious, and after dinner we played kissing games. This was the first time that Bev had French kissed me, and needless to say, I really enjoyed it. Kissing was as far as we progressed sexually, but I know I had more than platonic thoughts.

On Friday and Saturday nights, we often went to movies or we would just go for a walk together. We talked and talked about school, about our activities, and about how much fun we were having. One day as we lay in the park grass she told me she "wanted to be a pharmacist and get married and have a family." She said, "I love you and hope we can be together forever." I said, "I love you too" and "I want to become a pharmacologist and research new drugs." We tentatively planned to attend Idaho State University (ISU) together. Despite what we said to each other, I think we both knew that our relationship was a first relationship that probably would not last.

Bev and I continued our relationship right up until the time I was to leave for college. Instead of attending ISU, I decided to attend the University of Idaho in Moscow. Bev was saddened by this news, but I think she might have felt liberated, as well. We mutually decided to break up our relationship and give each other the freedom to start dating other people as soon as I left for college. We wrote letters back and forth for a few months and then we stopped writing. Sadly, we never saw each other again. Through friends, I learned that Bev attended Idaho State University in Pocatello, married, and had the family she dreamed about.

Graduation from high school was a bigger life change than I had anticipated. People had told me that after graduation I would not see most of the people in my high school ever again. That seemed unfathomable to my young mind. Yet it turned out to be true: after graduation, I only saw my immediate friends and a few other people again . . . ever.

Like most high school graduations of that era, there was a "secret" beer party taking place in a "secret" remote location along the Snake River near Firth, Idaho, one evening. Almost every senior made plans to attend that beer party. My friends and I arrived at about ten p.m. Already it was a raucous event. There were thirty to forty cars full of celebrating seniors and several kegs of beer. Within just a few minutes of our arrival, the police arrived and everyone piled in their cars and sped away in all directions from the scene. We spent the rest of the night just driving around and looking for any activity, but we found none, and in the light of morning drove home realizing that our graduation night was a bust.

# CHAPTER THREE:
# COLLEGE LIFE

College was a grand adventure in which I would have an opportunity to make new friends and to live with most of them. I decided to pledge a fraternity at the University of Idaho. One of the fraternity members, Dana, had contacted me during the summer and told me that by pledging, I would have a much better college experience and that, most importantly, the fraternities had the best access to the sorority girls, the most attractive girls on campus. Dana was an older graduate of Idaho Falls High School and also my hero. He was handsome, popular, drove a new Corvette, and his parents owned the local ski resort.

Going through rush was super fun—each fraternity was trying to impress, so they gave free parties with unlimited free food and beverages. I had never been exposed to so much alcohol in my life. In Idaho Falls, we were sheltered and I had only consumed one beer by the time of graduation. During rush week all the members of each fraternity house were as phony nice as they could be. At the end of rush week, I selected Pi Kappa Alpha, and they selected me as a pledge.

My college life was the opposite of high school. Suddenly, I was surrounded by temptations in the form of girls, booze, and drugs. (I quickly learned that the University of Idaho led the nation in per capita alcohol consumption in 1967, according to *Playboy* magazine.) For twenty-four hours a day, nobody but me was responsible for my behavior. My new fraternity brothers supplied a false Idaho driver's license that said I was twenty-one years old, though I was only eighteen. Those temptations and freedom, plus the influence of new fraternity brothers as friends, were almost my undoing. My hormones, like those of my fraternity brothers, were raging, and girls were the first, second, and third priority. We were constantly trying to meet new girls and hoping to "get lucky." I started drinking heavily like almost all of my friends. Fortunately, they didn't experiment with drugs and I chose not to experiment, as well. This decision was made during a time in which LSD was readily available at the University of Idaho.

Despite the fact that we had mandatory study table for two to three hours per day in the fraternity, my grades started to spiral downward. By the end of my freshman year, my grades had fallen below a C average. My fraternity friends were not helping my cause, but I alone was making the poor decisions that were hurting me scholastically.

Physical fraternity hazing had been outlawed by the time I attended college. But mental hazing was still permitted and was in widespread use. All of us Pi Kappa Alpha pledges knew that a vote was taken at the end of the semester to determine whether or not each pledge would become a member. A covered bag was passed and each member would secretly drop in either a white or black ball. We were told throughout our year as pledges that just one member could black ball any pledge and that pledge would not be allowed to remain in the fraternity.

The last week of being a pledge was called "Hell Week" for a reason. During Hell Week, fraternity members went so far as to implement brainwashing techniques used by the Chinese communists on prisoners of war. Pledges were subjected to sleep deprivation, food rationing, grueling physical work schedules, disgusting tasks, and constant mental harassment. The goal of all this hazing was to create a feeling of shared adversity and therefore a heightened feeling of "brotherhood" for those who endured. To me, the hazing was an outdated and silly ritual. But I tolerated it, as did my fellow pledge class members, and in the end, all the pledges in my class were accepted as members.

Fraternity activities were about 20 percent mature and 80 percent immature, which perhaps reflected the age of the members and the fact that, after all, it was the 1960s. In many ways our fraternity was very similar to the one portrayed in the movie *Animal House*. We had many of the same characters, we enjoyed toga parties, and we often rode around on our restored, chain-drive, 1927 Seagrave fire engine. We also had formal "serenades" in which we would dress in coats and ties and go sing to the women of a particular sorority. The songs were very proper and the whole exercise was to show we were gentlemen. We did community projects in which we would clean up a park, help with vaccinations, or help build a community center. And we had study hall and competitions for good grades both within our fraternity and against other houses that were intended to improve our study habits.

But most of the time, we also had weekly parties, "pre-functions," "post-functions," and "porchings." Pre-functions were drinking parties before an event, such as a dance or a game, and post-functions were drinking parties after a similar event. Porchings involved a few hours of embarrassing hazing directed at anyone who was recently engaged or who had pinned a girl. The porching victim would be stripped to their underwear and tied spread eagle to a mattress. Then various foul liquids like coffee grounds and mustard would be smeared on their skin. The unfortunate victims of this barbaric ritual would then be paraded outside in public and their fraternity brothers would yell derisive comments. Alcohol was consumed very heavily and our behavior much of the time was disgusting to older adults.

The sixty-plus men and boys in the fraternity were more or less randomly selected by circumstance. We wouldn't necessarily have chosen each other as friends. Living in the fraternity was somewhat like being in the military because I was required to get along with strangers in a living situation. We all slept together in "sleeping porches," large rooms full of many sets of bunk beds. To avoid a mass suffocation, the local fire code required that the sleeping porches have windows open at all times. In the winter snow would enter and settle on our blankets. Needless to say, the cold conditions made electric blankets essential.

In the process of sleeping, eating, and living with sixty-plus other brothers, we learned a great deal about everyone and about ourselves. The greater our collective challenges were, the more we bonded. With time, we did thrive as friends, and many of my fraternity brothers are still friends today.

In the fall of 1968, our fraternity house was condemned by the city. Fraternity members who were living on campus were moved to Shoup Hall. During rush week that fall, my fraternity brother friend George and I came up with an excellent plan for meeting girls. We would greet new female arrivals at the sororities and the dorms and offer to help them move all their stuff from their cars into the sorority or the dorm. This "help them move in" plan worked so well we were sorry we hadn't thought of it sooner. It was fun meeting new girls and we learned many things in helping them.

As a result of this activity, George and I soon knew literally hundreds of girls. Immediately we were both going out on dates with new girls every night of the week. My connections with the campus female population got me elected to the position of fraternity social chairman, a job I came to adore. Each weekend I was responsible for getting dates for any new pledges or other members that didn't have dates. I liked to call around to the sororities and flirt with the girls.

I learned some lessons from my friends in the fraternity that would be important to my life. One was the lesson of having good manners. I learned both in my fraternity and as a "hasher" serving food in various sororities how a table should be properly set. I learned the proper use of napkins. I learned how to eat like a gentleman and most of the rules for table manners. Because I knew the rules, I also learned how to be relaxed in a formal eating environment.

The second lesson I learned was that of music appreciation. One of the older members, Ray, was a drum musician. Ray inspired in me a love of music and particularly a love of jazz. He got me interested in the Dave Brubeck Quartet and other groups and musicians. I owe him many hours of pleasure from music appreciation.

The third lesson I learned was the importance of romantic love. My pledge brother and best friend, Joe, decided to marry his high school sweetheart from Grangeville. Together Joe and I had long talks about whether or not he was ready to be married. He said that he was ready because when he was with this woman, "The good times are twice as good and the bad times are half as bad." I never forgot those words, and later they helped me to make the correct decision about my future wife.

Never in my life have I been a better friend than I was as a child and teen in the 1960s. Most of each day was devoted to friends. I learned by trial and error how to better choose my friends and how to better maintain my friendships. With time, I learned to be less selfish and more giving. I learned to focus on the good in others. Smiling put me in a better place to be a friend. I also learned to forgive my friends. Slowly, I learned to be a positive mirror for others. I learned to help my friends. I learned to be kind to them.

Many of my friendship skills were put on the back burner during later years. I didn't fully appreciate my friends and instead concentrated my attention on my family, my education, and my work. For that, I have lost many friends over the years, something I deeply regret. After 2010, I realized my friendships were too closely tied to my career and to my status as one half of a "married couple." When my job ended and my wife died that year, I allowed many of my friendships to die too. The saying "you don't know what you've got till it's gone" became painfully apparent when many of my friends vanished. The loneliness I felt then helped me to realize the importance of friends in a more profound way. Today, I am still learning to appreciate my friends and to be thankful for the light they give to my life.

The value of friendship is a simple idea, but it is also a profound truth. We know in our heart of hearts that having friends is good for us. They help us celebrate the joy of living and they make our good times better. Friends also help us make the bad times less bad and they pick us up when we are down. We can endure all the pains in life more effectively with friends.

Our friendships also have a powerful impact on our physical health. A lack of social connection can be as damaging as smoking, drinking too much, or living a sedentary lifestyle. Friendships can improve our mood, help us to reach our goals, reduce our stress and depression, support us through tough times, support us as we age, and boost our sense of self-worth. Even our longevity is tied to the quality of our friendships.

In the decade of the 1960s, I learned that in order to have good friends,

I must invest my time and energy to *be* a good friend. The benefits of friendship were both immediate and long-term. Having friends gave me practice to live and work with others more effectively. Friends encouraged me to be more active and athletic, which produced long-term physical and emotional benefits. I learned that communicating with friends helped me to understand the world more completely. I remain very grateful for all of my friends.

In March of 1969, I met the girl of my dreams—but it took me a little while to realize that she was the one for me. As social chairman, I was the person in charge of our annual Dream Girl Dance, which always occurred on the weekend closest to March 1. Every year our fraternity would select six to twelve women to compete for the title of "Dream Girl," a kind of miss popularity contest in which all the members voted for the girl whom they liked the most. The winner was announced at the formal dance.

We all had dates to the dance, and before the dance, we held a pre-function. I met Susan Clark for the first time at that pre-function. Susan was the date of another pledge from my fraternity. I had my own date (whose name, funny enough, I don't remember). For me there certainly was an element of cupidity in the air that night. Susan and I kept ignoring our dates and flirting with each other in the kitchen. We kept finding excuses to go back for more snacks or to refresh our drinks. I immediately connected with Susan in a hundred ways. Despite the immediate connection, I thought it improper for me to ask her out until I had clearance from my fraternity brother.

In 1969, our fraternity had our evening meals at the cafeteria of the Theophilus Tower. Susan worked in the cafeteria serving food and wiping up the tables. She sometimes wore an alluring leather miniskirt. For many days, I saw her working and said hi.

Finally, in May of 1969, we went out on our first date together. It was on a Thursday night. We liked each other so much that we went out on both Friday and Saturday nights, as well. For the remainder of May, Susan and I were together always: playing tennis, sunbathing, going for picnics, going for drives, picking wildflowers, tossing a softball, going to parties, and going to the movies. In less than a month, we had become best friends and lovers.

We had secret intimate names for each other. I called Susan "Pookey" and she called me "Patter." We used those names for more than forty years—all the time we were together. We weren't very secretive about our love for each other; we exhibited almost constant PDAs (public displays of affection). Our favorite PDA was holding hands. Our second favorite was kissing. We had many other PDAs that I won't discuss in detail here.

It was difficult to say goodbye to Susan when school ended that summer. I was working as an engineering aid for the Forest Service in the Nez Perce Forest on the Selway River and Susan was working in Boise. I made two trips to Boise to see Susan during the summer, and we both wrote love letters back and forth. We giddily anticipated being back together at the University of Idaho in the fall.

When fall came, Susan and I started dating again, and for a period, our romance blossomed. But after Thanksgiving, we experienced some communication problems and I became very jealous when Susan started dating other guys. Finally, in December I said, "I don't want you dating anyone except me. I seriously love you. It makes me crazy when you go on dates with other guys." Susan replied, "I love you too. I had no idea, and I am so sorry I hurt you." With tears in her eyes she said, "I will only date you, Patter. I really do love you." From that moment forward, we were destined to become one. Our mutual love grew stronger and stronger the next year. Our story together would continue in the next decade: the 1970s.

# The 1970s:

## Family is Everything

"The only rock I know that stays steady, the only institution I know that works, is the family."

**—Lee Iacocca**

# CHAPTER FOUR: A YOUNG MARRIED COUPLE

In August of 1970 I married Susan Clark, the first true love of my life. We began a new life as a couple—a single unit—and together we set a course to build a strong family. We began the decade as newlyweds and ended it as a family of our own. Together, we experienced the joy of marriage, the glory of childbirth, the excitement of raising children, and the various challenges of life.

We were young, in love, and full of energy to solve the many problems of youth and naïveté that we faced. For us, the seventies was a decade of investment. We invested our energy in our own education, our mutual love and respect, and in our children. We provided a safe environment for our family to grow. Both in the 1970s and today, I continue loving, respecting, and growing our family.

It was in April of 1970 that I proposed marriage to Susan. Before my proposal, I tested the waters and mentioned that, "someday when we're married, we will . . ." Susan was hypersensitive to marriage talk and she instructed me, "You should not talk that way unless you really mean it!" "I *do* mean it," I replied. "I'm serious."

A few weeks later, I made my formal proposal. We were out on a date, and as the date was winding down, we found ourselves alone together in the car. I decided to make my proposal on one knee in the "old-school" style. I opened my door and got down on one knee. I said, "My dear Susan, I love you completely. I want to dedicate my life to you. Will you please marry me?" Susan started crying. Through tears of joy, she said, "Yes! Yes! Yes! Oh I love you, too, Patter!"

As we went together the following day to shop for rings, a complex mix of emotions swirled inside me. I was elated that we were getting married, and at the same time I was frightened because we were so young. I thought to myself, "How will I support us? And how can I even pay for our rings?" We decided to have our wedding close to the end of the summer so we could earn as much money as possible working at our summer jobs.

August 29, 1970, seemed like the perfect Saturday for a wedding. My mother surprised us both by giving us the diamond from her engagement ring. We incorporated the diamond from my mother's ring in a new setting for Sue's engagement ring. My mother's gift meant a great deal to Susan and to me. It meant that she really did give us her blessing.

We knew Sue's mother would insist that we get married in the Weiser Christian Church, so we planned to hold both the wedding and reception there. We didn't have enough money for a real honeymoon, so we planned a single night in a Boise hotel before starting life together in our new trailer house in Boise. We would have our honeymoon later.

During the summer of 1970, Susan was working as a lifeguard for the Idaho State Department of Parks at Sandy Point on the Boise River below Lucky Peak Dam. I worked again as an engineering aid for the US Forest Service at Fenn Ranger Station in the Nez Perce National Forest in north central Idaho. My job was to count and record the daily numbers of belly-dump rock trucks and to supervise the location where each one dumped their loads during the construction of logging roads in the forest. My job was not very taxing and allowed me ample time to read books and eat huckleberries.

Susan and I had many opportunities to get together during the summer. I went to visit her in Boise and she came to see me at Fenn Ranger Station. We were deeply in love and wrote many love letters back and forth— many sweet words resonant with passion and affection. In July, when Susan discovered she was pregnant, we were both ecstatic. We knew that her parents would be "disappointed in our behavior," but we both wanted a family and were happy that our first child would come very soon after we were married. We loved each other very deeply and we loved this child that would come the following spring. In our unabashed excitement, we wanted to fast forward time and get to our wedding as soon as possible.

Just one week before the wedding, I traveled to Weiser to be baptized. I had been baptized before as a young child, but Susan's mother, Christabel, did not trust a sprinkling baptism to have the proper effect. In her church only immersion baptisms were considered proper. So, rather than cause a family argument before the wedding, I conceded to be baptized again in the Weiser Christian Church. The baptism went smoothly and was over in a few minutes.

But other things did not progress so smoothly. On the evening before our wedding, Susan became very angry over her mother's meddling. Christabel had planned every tiny detail of the wedding and Susan put up with a lack of control as long as she could. Finally, she couldn't continue to be tolerant. Susan threw an enormous fit, but neither parent tried to assuage her. Instead, they came to me and said, "She usually isn't like this." They were both concerned that I would change my mind at the last minute. They need not have worried! I was amused at the battle between Susan and her mother, but I was also deeply in love and would have gone forward with our marriage regardless of the events the night before. I knew that Sue's emotions were high that evening and she was just reacting to the stress of her mother's wedding orchestration.

The next afternoon, our wedding ceremony was about to begin. Everyone asked me if I was nervous. I said, "No, I am perfectly calm. Why?" They pointed out that I was wearing Susan's father's suit coat rather than my own. After I realized they were right, I was both embarrassed and nervous.

Despite my nerves, we had a beautiful wedding. Susan wore a classic white wedding dress and the bridesmaids were clad in yellow and green, our wedding colors. We recorded audio of the wedding, which went swimmingly, on a small, reel-to-reel tape—the best available technology for the time. The ladies of the church prepared a nice reception meal in the basement after the service. The day was perfect and Susan and I were euphoric.

We moved into a new trailer house, twelve feet wide and fifty feet long, that we were paying for with monthly payments. It cost $4,700 for the new trailer and our payments were about $75 per month. The trailer park space at Owyhee Trailer Village cost $50 per month (the highest in Boise). This brought our total rent to $125 per month—fairly high rent for young newlyweds. To pay our rent and buy food, Susan began working as a clerk at the Grand Central store on Fairview and I started as an assistant manager at the 7-Eleven on the corner of Roosevelt and Overland. Sue and I loved our young family life, but we didn't get as much time together as we wanted because we both worked at least forty hours per week and our shifts seldom coincided. Still, as time passed, we grew even closer as a couple and our love for each other grew stronger, as well.

We still faced the daily challenges of life. One day, I was fired from my job, the only time in my life I have been fired. The Southland Corporation (the owner of 7-Eleven stores) decided to close the store where I was the assistant manager because there just wasn't enough business coming into the store. Management decided that they could only retain one full-time person by transferring them to a new store. My store manager selected himself for the transfer. That meant that he had to fire me.

The news angered Sue greatly. She was so irate that she went with me back to the store and yelled at my former manager for about thirty minutes. I loved Susan even more that day! My now ex-manager admitted that I was a good worker and that I had done a good job but said he had to fire me so that 7-Eleven wouldn't have to pay the resultant benefits from a layoff. Sue and I were naïve and we were afraid to hire a lawyer and fight for our rights, so we let it go.

Within a week, I got a new job at Grand Central as an assistant manager in the camera bar and candy department. Working at Grand Central gave me more educational opportunity than 7-Eleven. Our department was responsible for wine and beer sales in addition to electronics and food, so I was required to complete the thirty-day California Wine Course to increase my knowledge of wines. I enjoyed the course and developed a greater appreciation for wine as a result. Like many other forms of education, my knowledge of wines has served me well throughout my life.

On March 18, 1971, I was working at Grand Central in Boise when Sue went into labor. My brother-in-law, Gary Nelson, called me to give me the news. Gary said not to hurry, that labor takes a long time, and he instructed me to relax and take my time. Right! I was too excited to relax. I dashed home and checked to see if Susan had left anything, then rushed to the hospital as fast as I could drive.

Upon my arrival, I raced to the information desk, explaining that my wife was having a baby, and asked them to direct me to the waiting room. "Ah . . . we don't do maternity here," they said. "Oops." I felt so stupid. I had driven to the wrong hospital! They directed me to the correct one, and I rushed back to my car and drove to St. Luke's Hospital.

They did indeed have a maternity ward, and, yes, Susan was there. In those days, fathers were not allowed in the delivery room, so I was directed to the waiting room. All of a sudden time stopped. I waited for about two hours but it seemed like ten. Tick tock. Tick tock. Tick tock . . .

Finally, a group of Lamaze students led by two doctors came into the room. They all stared at me, the expectant father. I was twenty-one years old but looked about fourteen. I remember being embarrassed by their stares. The doctors pointed out to the students that I looked nervous. They were right.

The waiting continued, but after another hour, one of the nurses told me that "all is going well." She lied. While I was waiting outside, the doctors were fighting to save Susan's life and the life of our baby. Susan's preeclampsia had not been diagnosed at any time during her pregnancy, and during the birth, she developed eclampsia that caused violent seizures and extremely high blood pressure. Preeclampsia happens because the placenta isn't functioning properly, but the specific cause of the condition is unknown. Thank God that Susan was so young and physically strong! Thank God that the doctors were able to safely deliver the baby and keep Susan alive!

Soon after the birth of Miquette Kim Cavanaugh, I was allowed to go in and see Susan and our new baby. There are no words to describe that moment. It was as if my life before that moment had not even happened, and my real life was just beginning. The love Susan and I had for each other and for our baby was at a peak that day. Even still, the very thought of it fills me with a deep, warm, ineffable feeling. Only those of you who have experienced the birth of a child will understand. It is a moment like no other.

Our baby was perfect. Our love for that baby was perfect. It was the completion of the circle of life, and Susan and I both realized in that moment how important that completion was. We also realized immediately that we loved this small human being in a way and in a capacity that we hadn't dreamed possible. This baby was a part of us—a part of us individually and a part of us as a couple. Our life was now changed. We would never be the same. This baby Miquette Kim (Micki) made us a family.

Susan and I had old fashioned, traditional ideas about family roles. We both believed that Sue should stay home as much as possible and raise the children and that I should be the person responsible for earning money. Susan loved being a mother and she became skilled in that role. My plan, meanwhile, was to save enough money to go back to college and finish my education so that I could earn money to support our family by myself. However, during my time in college, we were so poor that Susan had to work part time at Grand Central. Later, she provided childcare services for up to five very young children (all fewer than three years old). We tried to work our schedules so one of us was at home for Micki. Later, we hired another Boise State College (BSC) student named Kathy as a babysitter for Micki so we could both work at the same time.

After working at Grand Central for about one year, I had earned enough money to return to college at Boise State. I told the store manager at Grand Central that I wanted to work part time and return to college. He agreed to allow me a demotion to work part time as a regular employee.

Because my grades from the University of Idaho were poor, I began again as a provisional Boise State student and could only take a few classes. After a semester or two, I was allowed to enroll as a full-time student. Unsure as to whether I wanted to study geology or environmental health science, I left the decision to the flip of a coin. Geology it was. It turned out that geology was the perfect fit for me and my skills.

I learned very early on that geology was a combination of science and art. Geology required the precision of mathematics and concrete evidence like all the other sciences. It also required an ability to interpret between the lines and to artfully envision what had happened over millions of years from subtle clues. I loved both the scientific challenge of geology and the artistic challenge of looking at the world in a unique way. My hunting and fishing experience also gave me an advantage in geological fieldwork. I already knew how to operate a four-wheel-drive vehicle and I was comfortable living and working in remote deserts and forests. I excelled in college because I loved the intellectual challenge involved in learning about geologic processes.

Having a family effected a major transformation in my life and produced a sea change in my work ethic between my college years before marriage and after marriage. At the University of Idaho, I was attending college to have fun, chase girls, and to find myself as a person. I studied the minimum amount required to stay in school. At Boise State University (BSU), I had a purpose: to be the best husband and father I could be. This meant that I would do my best and work my hardest in college so that later I could provide for my family.

My newfound motivation showed in the results. I only received two Bs during my three years at Boise State; the rest of my grades were As. A serious student, I was well respected by both the professors and other students. I needed the strong work ethic I developed at Boise State to be successful later in graduate school.

Today I am very thankful for the close student friends I had while attending Boise State. Many became friends for life and I owe them much. The geology community at Boise State was like having an extended family. The professors were only a few years older than the students, so we all bonded nicely and became good friends. Dr. Ken Hollenbaugh, then geology department chairman at BSU, took me under his wing and helped me in many ways. He was a mentor throughout my undergraduate years at BSU, and we developed a strong friendship. Eventually, Dr. Hollenbaugh became the first dean of the graduate school, and our friendship continued for a long time.

During the school year, he helped me qualify for a work-study program that provided income in return for my work as a teaching assistant in geology labs. I taught physical geology and mineralogy labs and learned more about geology teaching the labs than I did as a student. The geology department acquired a Vreeland spectrophotometer, and Dr. Hollenbaugh put me in charge of operating the instrument. He also had me care for the Rodenbaugh mineral collection that had been donated to the university.

During the summer, he hired me as a geologic assistant for the Ada Council of Governments, working on his project to find a way to stabilize Warm Springs Mesa. The houses on Warm Springs Mesa had been construct-ed on a former landslide that had been reactivated when the residents started watering their lawns. All the houses had started to move. A few houses near the front of the slide had slid five to fifteen feet down the hill, and wide cracks had developed in some foundations.

A practical geologist, Dr. Hollenbaugh offered a useful solution in his report. He suggested that a number of gently upward sloping holes be drilled from the toe of the slide and into the rock and soil just above the glide plane under the landslide. Then, perforated pipe was inserted into each hole. The effect of the pipe was to hold the hole open and to drain the water from the rock and soil before it reached the glide plane. This drainage action eliminated the lubrication on the glide plane despite heavy rains and constant watering by the residents. The technique worked very well and Warm Springs Mesa has remained stable to this day, forty-three years later.

While I was attending BSU, the college established the first chapter of Sigma Gamma Epsilon, the earth science honorary fraternity. My good grades allowed me to join Sigma Gamma Epsilon, and I was elected the first president of the Boise State chapter. It was an honor to serve as the chapter president and to host the first Earth Day celebration in Boise. We held the celebration on October 23, the day the Archbishop of Usher calculated was the day the earth was created through his careful reading of the Bible. Our Earth Day party received Boise television and newspaper coverage, and Susan was proud of my involvement. Our Earth Day celebration in Boise only lasted for a few years, and it should not be confused with the national Earth Day that began in 1970 and is now widely celebrated on either March 21 or April 22.

Although the professors at Boise State University were not as tech-nically sophisticated as those at other colleges, they did provide a good, solid educational base in geology. They also believed strongly in work experience for their graduates and they assisted every student in obtaining a summer job in geology. As a result, during the 1970s, every Boise State graduate in the geology department had at a minimum two summers of work experience by the time they graduated, facilitating their acquisition of employment following graduation.

During the summer of 1974, I was employed as a geologist for Cyprus Mines Corporation and was assigned to the Thompson Creek molybdenum project in central Idaho. Molybdenum is an element used as an alloy in the steel industry. We were drilling the Thompson Creek deposit to determine whether or not it could be economically mined. Our family lived in a trailer house on the Salmon River near Clayton, Idaho. Our daughter Micki relished being the only child and having her father's and mother's full-time attention. She was very cute when she would toddle to the adjacent store and buy candy. On the one occasion in which she forgot to pay, we took her back to the store and had her apologize and then pay for her treats. She still remembers being embarrassed by her parents that day.

I worked as a "core logger," recording the rock type, alteration, mineralization, and fracturing for drill core from the Thompson Creek deposit. I learned a great deal about mineral exploration and about managing people from my boss. Bob was an engineer who had managed many people on expensive projects, such as New York subway tunnel construction, and he was skilled at extracting the maximum effort from everyone. His "paying-it-forward" management technique involved asking each individual how much they wanted to be paid to do a job, and then giving them a little more than they requested. Bob expected people would later return the favor and give him a little extra when it was necessary to keep the project running smoothly. Bob's management style was so effective that I employed many elements of that style as a manager later in my career.

The Forest Service required that an Environmental Impact Study (EIS) be completed before the Thompson Creek molybdenum deposit could be mined. In order to complete the EIS, a team of biologists had to evaluate the impact of the mine on the animals and write a report. Cyprus hired a consulting firm to complete the evaluation. The consultant biologists grew up and lived in the eastern United States and therefore had little knowledge about western animal and plant species. We locals had to tell them about the various species of plants, animals, and fish living near the mine site.

To understand the impact of the mine on the ground squirrel population, the biologists captured thousands of the creatures in live traps. To mark the captured ground squirrels, they cut the claws off the feet. The plan was to recapture squirrels the following year and make counts of the differing numbers of marked and unmarked individuals. There was a significant problem with the study: all the ground squirrels having cut claws died. None were captured the following year because the act of cutting the claws killed the squirrels. So the environmental study itself caused the greatest impact in the ground squirrel population.

The summer after I graduated from Boise State (1975), I was very fortunate to find employment as an exploration geologist for the minerals division of Conoco in their copper porphyry exploration program. The geologists who became my friends and mentors that summer were a group of men who were all-star explorationists, some of the best in the industry. Collectively, these three geologists had more knowledge of metals exploration than pretty much any other three people. I learned a tremendous amount about mineral exploration in Nevada from these mentors during that summer—certainly more than I had learned throughout undergraduate school at Boise State. I became skilled at geologic mapping, recognizing alteration types, and recognizing subtle copper gossans, valuable knowledge that I would take with me to graduate school and on to my career. More importantly, I made a number of excellent contacts and friends in the exploration business.

Although we desperately needed the money from immediate employment, Susan and I made the decision together to invest in our family's long-term future and continue my education in graduate school. I had applied at both the University of Montana in Missoula, Montana, and at the New Mexico Institute of Mining and Technology in Socorro, New Mexico. I was admitted to the graduate program at the University of Montana on the basis of my high GRE scores in mathematics. We needed as much financial help as possible for me to attend graduate school, but thankfully, I was granted a TA, or teaching assistantship, at the University of Montana. This meant we didn't have to borrow money to pay for grad school.

When I arrived at the University of Montana, I discovered that it was a rather academic/cerebral college. My professors in Missoula were generally distant and aloof. Most had written the books we were studying and were considered giants in the field of geology. Several were big-name researchers who had little time for teaching. Most of the other professors were not big names, but they were just as focused and it was difficult to form friendships with them.

For this and other reasons, graduate school was a very different experience when compared with my undergraduate education. At BSU, I was one of the top students. At the University of Montana, my geologic knowledge was anemic when compared with the knowledge of my fellow grad students who had been educated in more prestigious institutions. I worked very hard to compete with them. Moreover, we grad students had a huge daily homework load, and I was required to teach labs much of each day. I taught physical geology, mineralogy, and engineering geology labs. Again, I learned a great deal from teaching the labs and from my fellow grad students.

Because almost all of my energy had to be devoted to graduate school, Susan had to keep the home front going alone much of the time. Our family was a partnership. She was responsible for caring for Micki and for providing the bulk of the family income. Susan, Micki, and I lived a very frugal life during graduate school in Missoula. Susan made about $400 per month income by driving a school bus for the owner of our trailer park. We received an additional $300 per month from my teaching assistantship. Altogether, it was barely enough to pay the trailer park lot rental fee and to buy food. For many months, we lived on beans, rice, tea, and milk. One glorious day we won a $500 gift certificate for groceries at a local supermarket. Then we were able to enjoy a few food indulgences like ice cream and steak. Despite our financial struggles during grad school in Missoula, we were happy, healthy, working hard on our future, and enveloped in romantic and familial love.

# CHAPTER FIVE: OUR WHITE CLOUD ADVENTURE

One of my duties as a graduate student was to complete a master's thesis. The professors at the University of Montana put an emphasis on doing "good science" in the thesis. Their goal was the advancement of geologic understanding. My goal as a starving grad student with a family was to do a thesis that provided an economic benefit. The professors and my fellow grad students called me a mercenary and made fun of my concern with the economic value of my work. Nevertheless, I was determined to get my thesis work paid for by somebody.

I kept my eyes open and my ears to the ground. Then, at the annual Northwest Mining Association convention in Spokane, I learned about an opportunity. The district manager for the American Smelting and Refining Company (ASARCO) gave a talk on exploration during which he mentioned that ASARCO sometimes funded a master's thesis on one of their projects by hiring students as camp caretakers.

I contacted the ASARCO manager and visited him at his office in Spokane, explaining that I was interested in doing a thesis on the Little Boulder Creek molybdenum deposit in Idaho. He was very frank with me. He told me that he had literally hundreds of applications for each position and stated that he wouldn't even *read* resumes from students attending the University of Montana because the professors there were so politically liberal. I convinced him to ignore the fact that I was a student in Missoula. I argued that my industry experience trumped my college experience and affirmed my support for ASARCO's goals. In the end, the manager relented and agreed to hire me and fund my master's thesis on the Little Boulder Creek deposit.

In the summer of 1976, Susan and I embarked on one of the most treasured adventures of our lives. We were ferried by helicopter to the White Cloud mountain range in central Idaho to become caretakers at ASARCO's mining camp and to do fieldwork on my master's thesis. The camp was located eight miles from the nearest road in the newly created Sawtooth National Recreation Area (SNRA). The SNRA was created as a response to the controversy over proposed mining of the Little Boulder Creek molybdenum deposit by ASARCO. My thesis project would be to study the geology of that famous and controversial ore deposit. Each summer for the prior six years ASARCO had funded a thesis project in the White Cloud mountain area. None of the other six graduate students had completed their thesis. They had been distracted by the freedom and beauty of the SNRA. I was determined to be different and finish my thesis.

Baker Lake view from our cabin in the White Cloud Mountains, 1976

The ASARCO manager was concerned that Susan and I were young and unprepared for living in the wilderness. He didn't appreciate the fact that because we had been hunting, fishing, camping, and working in remote forests for much of our lives, we felt very comfortable and safe living in the SNRA and taking care of the mining camp. Initially, Susan and I were instructed that we would have to leave our daughter behind, so we had my parents in Idaho Falls babysit Micki for the first month while we lived in the White Clouds. After we proved our mettle in the wilderness, we were allowed to have our daughter join us. Micki arrived by helicopter with my sister, Mary. Our daughter was wide-eyed and very afraid when she stepped off the helicopter. I had begun to grow a beard and she did not recognize me. But Micki relaxed and became our daughter again when she finally realized we really were her parents.

For the three of us, living in the White Clouds was like living in paradise. From our camp, we enjoyed a view of the glacier-carved Baker Lake in the foreground and the 11,815 feet-high Castle Peak in the background. This view made the cover of the Sierra Club calendar that year. Although we lived at 8,600 feet elevation in the SNRA, we were provided with restaurant-quality cooking facilities, hot and cold running water, refrigerators, freezers, chopped firewood, and electricity. Every two or three weeks we could order whatever food and beverages our hearts desired and our order would be brought to us by helicopter—all for free. We had steaks and crab and shrimp in the freezer and beer stacked in cases high along our windows.

There were some minor inconveniences too. It was an adventure learning how to maintain the diesel generator and our marine band radio. Most of the time we could talk back and forth with Mountain Messaging in Boise. The call sign we used was "KOH 646, this is unit 21." Boise was more than one hundred miles away, so the radio's utility was subject to solar activity and other factors. We used a single one hundred-feet-long copper wire tied between trees and stretched perpendicular to the direction of Boise as our antenna.

Like her father (and her grandfather before that), Micki learned to be an excellent fisherman because I would help her fish in Baker Lake and the outflow almost every day. She loved catching the cutthroat trout, Eastern brook trout, and bull trout. For a short period, Micki kept a pet grasshopper named Edie. When Edie died, she put him on a hook to catch a fish.

One day a group of boy scouts rode horses up the trail and camped on Baker Lake. I watched as the twenty-five teenaged boys tried to catch the elusive trout in the lake and outflow stream. They had no success and were making comments about how terrible the fishing seemed to be. Quietly I told Micki to go and get her fishing pole. In just a few minutes, while the older boy scouts watched in amazement, five-year-old Micki pulled a half dozen fish from the lake and stream. We cooked them for dinner that evening and Micki was very proud of her fishing prowess.

While our family was living in the White Clouds, we became concerned for our safety, so we borrowed a pet dog named Orogeny ("Rog") from some friends in Missoula. Rog was a massive black German Shepard. Rog's power and size made him an excellent protector. We wanted him in our cabin in case a bear decided to join us for dinner. In fact, the winter before our arrival, a ravenous black bear destroyed the wall to our cookhouse and then he squeezed every can in storage to make it pop until he forced the contents out. He then smelled the spillage and devoured only the contents he liked. Knowing that a bear could come through the wall any time was sobering. Fortunately, we saw no bears during our summer in the White Clouds.

It was a frightening adventure taking Rog in the glass bubble of the Bell helicopter and watching him panic as the ground slipped away from under the bubble. Rog jumped and struggled while trying to get away from the ground falling under his feet. It was all we could do to grab him and try to wrestle him until we landed. Our pilot was not pleased to have a wildly behaving dog in the cockpit.

Bell Helicopter with Susan and our groceries headed for our camp in
the White Cloud Mountains.

When Rog had an encounter with a porcupine, his powerful jaws became a liability. Rog had discovered the porcupine about a half-mile from our camp, chased it down, and took a big bite. We heard his barks and painful yowls and knew that something terrible had happened.

The poor dog ended up with more than two hundred quills embedded in his mouth, sixty quills in his tongue alone. He whimpered in pain and foam ran constantly from his mouth. Susan and I took turns holding the dog while the other one pulled quills out of his mouth with pliers. Quill pulling and quill cutting was a slow and difficult process that lasted the remainder of the day and into the night. Somehow, Rog knew that bearing the pain was his only option. Nevertheless, he was patient and did not bite us. Rog survived, and he learned his lesson not to bite another porcupine.

In late July, Susan's high school girlfriends from Weiser decided to ride their horses up to our camp. The Weiser women started their trip a little later than they intended and encountered some delays en route to the trailhead. Once they arrived at the trailhead on Little Boulder Creek, they made a rookie mistake that might have cost them their lives.

They arrived at about six fifteen p.m. with their horses, and by the time everything was unloaded and the horses were saddled, it was already seven p.m. and the sun was low on the horizon. The young ladies did not bring any sleeping bags or blankets. Despite the late hour, they made a bad decision to ride the horses up the trail towards our camp, unaware that the trail was so rocky and treacherous that it would take at least four or five hours to complete. These young women did not have any source of artificial illumination with them, and the new moon deprived the landscape of light by which to navigate, so by nine thirty p.m., the darkness was complete.

About halfway up the mountains, it became so dark outside that the ladies could not safely continue. Thankfully, they stopped, stayed on the horses, and unsuccessfully tried to sleep in the saddle. They were wearing summer clothing and the temperature began to drop near freezing at that elevation. The body heat radiating from the horses might have saved their lives. They spent the night shivering together and waiting desperately for daybreak.

Once the light returned the next morning, they continued up the trail. When they finally arrived at our campsite, they were some very cold and tired women. But they survived their mistake and no horses had been injured along the trail. We had them tie up the horses in the forest away from all our water sources. Then the ladies could finally take a hot shower. They warmed themselves in our kitchen near our wood cook stove and recounted the story of their perilous trip. After eating a hot breakfast, they all retired to warm beds in our workmen's cabins. The story of their ill-conceived ride has been retold many times in our family as an example of a bad decision with a fortunate result.

During the summer, we had no radio, no television, no telephone, no newspapers, and no magazines. In spite of, or perhaps because of, our isolation from civilization, it was the best summer of our lives.

When the summer ended, ASARCO paid to have the helicopter fly my 1,100 pounds of rock samples back to our car. They also paid for the cutting of thin sections, staining of rocks, drafting of my maps, and the typing of my thesis. It was a dream job and a dream thesis project.

# CHAPTER SIX: OUR
# FAMILY GROWS

On August 11, 1977, Susan gave birth to our second daughter, Alisha Brooke Cavanaugh, in Missoula, Montana. This pregnancy went very smoothly and Susan did not develop any significant problems. This time I was allowed to be in the delivery room for the birth of our daughter. And I was allowed to more closely experience the pain of childbirth with my loving wife. Finally, I felt the joy of seeing my perfect daughter as soon as she was delivered. That moment of delivery is still tied with the moment I saw my first daughter as one of the best moments of my life. Again, I felt the total love of being a new father to this perfect being and at the same time a husband to a loving wife and father to another perfect daughter. It was a feeling of being completed. It was a feeling that our new family was everything.

During the summer of 1976, I was employed as an exploration geologist in southwestern Montana. My employer was Utah International, and I worked with two talented and well-respected explorationists. Utah International geologists strictly followed the geological mapping standards adopted by the US Geological Survey. Certain geologic units always had to have the official patterns and colors so anyone in the company could quickly interpret the maps. For example, limestone units were always colored blue, and if they were dolomitic, they would be a darker blue. However, the emphasis on doing quality geology and having good form at the expense of results stymied Utah International's success, and despite producing perfect maps and well-written reports, the geologists made no significant discoveries. Still, I learned a considerable amount about the geology of western Montana. The two geologists were very good friends and both later attended my thesis presentation in Missoula.

By the summer of 1978, I had competed all of my coursework for my MS degree in geology. I still had to finish my thesis, but it was time to get a job and start to better support my family. I applied for many geological positions all over the United States but received only two immediate job offers. The first was a position with the US Army Corps of Engineers doing dam foundation investigations in Kansas City, Missouri. This job held little appeal to me.

The second job offer was to be a temporary geologist working on a one-year program for Burlington Northern Railroad (BN) in their coal and minerals division in Billings, Montana. I took the BN offer because at least it allowed our family to stay in Montana. Soon, we obtained a small U-Haul truck and loaded our belongings. We sold our trailer house in Missoula, and with the money from that sale plus $2,500 borrowed from my parents, we qualified to purchase a new house in Billings under the FHA 235 program. The 235 program provided federal subsidization of the interest, or a portion of the interest, on a new home. The program was income based, and my low starting salary of $800 per month allowed us to qualify. By the time we arrived in Billings, my temporary job had become a full-time job with Burlington Northern as a staff geologist.

While living in Billings, I still needed to complete my thesis to earn my master's degree. After two years and an untold number of drafts, edits, and sleepless nights, the thesis was approved. Now I just had to present and defend my thesis orally. As the day approached, I got very nervous. I was concerned that the faculty's questions would be too difficult or that my nerves would get the best of me and I would blank out. Finally, on the day of my oral presentation, I was happy to see three of my industry friends in the audience, as well as many professors and fellow grad students. I think my presentation went fairly well, but the faculty's questions were a disappointment. All of the good questions came from my industry friends, and it appeared that the faculty members were intimidated. None of the professors (including my thesis advisor) really understood economic geology and mineral exploration well enough to ask practical questions. Afterward, I realized that on the topic of the geology of the Little Boulder Creek Molybdenum Deposit, I was now the expert, and my confidence as an explorationist grew.

As the decade ended, Susan and I were working hard together to continue to build a loving family in our new home in Billings. Our daughters were our pride and joy. Micki now preferred to be called by her middle name of Kim. As Kim and Alisha grew, our love for them continued to grow. Susan was happy being a full-time stay-at-home mother. She loved the role of mother and I was very glad to have her in that role. Our seamless partnership continued to hold.

Young Cavanaugh family. Left to right in back row: Susan, Patrick, Kim. Front: Alisha.

The world can be a difficult place. Sometimes we need a safety net as we teeter across the tightrope of life. We require the help of others who love us and support us no matter what happens. We need a family. A secure family requires the investment of time and energy by all members. Each day we have to choose to love each other, respect each other, and be kind to each other.

Family can be thought of as a living organism in which individual family members are the veins and arteries, the beating heart and breathing lungs that supply life to that being. Each one is necessary to and strengthens the living whole. In an ideal family, extended members like one's parents, children,

children's spouses, and their offspring live in close proximity to each other. A family supports beliefs and traditions reinforced through the generations and tested by time. These beliefs and traditions help us know how to bond with each other, behave in the presence of others, and behave in a civilized society. In a loving family, children learn to love and respect their parents and parents learn to love and respect their children. A strong family has open and effective communication at its core, and each member is accepted as they are.

In America, our families have changed since the 1970s. No longer are split families, single-parent families, and blended families the exception; now they are the norm. Still, we would all ideally want our grandchildren to experience a loving family with two parents. We know instinctively that a two-parent family best provides the support we all need in this increasingly complex world. A loving family is still our collective goal.

Tom Wolfe named the 1970s the "Me Decade" because it was a time in which people turned inward, having grown tired of politics and tired especially of the Vietnam War. They were frustrated that the government would not listen to the majority and end that unpopular war. People in the United States gave up on politics and became more interested in themselves and in their families. The 1970s was also a decade of extreme behaviors. Fashion adopted strange color combinations. Some people purchased Pet Rocks or took up streaking (running naked in public). Others like Bill Gates and Steve Jobs became entrepreneurs and started new technologies.

Susan and I together built our lucky lives on the rock of being a loving family whose core was our relationship as husband and wife. Our relationship was not perfect—we had our disagreements and occasional arguments—but we tried to never go to bed while we were still angry. And we tried to refresh our love for each other as often as possible.

At the end of the decade, we experienced a marriage encounter weekend together. As a follow-up to the marriage encounter, we formed a "love circle" group with our neighborhood friends. For more than eight years, this group met weekly to learn and relearn how to communicate in our marriage.

As our communication skills improved, so did our relationship. Our strong partnership would be rewarded in the next decades: the 1980s, 1990s, and 2000s.

# The 1980s:

## It's Important to Love Your Work

"Your work is going to fill a large part of your life, and the only way to be truly satisfied is to do what you believe is great work. The only way to do what you believe is great work is to love what you do."

*—Steve Jobs*

# CHAPTER SEVEN: MY EARLY CAREER

The 1980s were a decade of political conservatism and the rise of the yuppies. During most of the decade, the Regan administration controlled the White House. Following the OPEC-created "oil crisis" in 1979, the US economy regained its footing and slowly began to soar. The Dow Jones industrial average more than tripled from 838 in the beginning of 1980 to 2,634 at the end of 1989. Military spending rose to $34 million per hour. Changes in the Soviet Union brought an end to the Cold War and the fall of the Berlin Wall. The Internet was developed in the 1980s and MTV began broadcasting. I discovered that the conservative political environment of the 1980s was the perfect decade in which to begin a gold exploration business.

Geology became my passion and my principal focus in life as soon as I started studying it in college. I loved the challenging geological mysteries: How did the earth form? What is the long-term heat balance of the earth? How did life on this and other planets begin? What causes the magnetic poles to reverse polarity? Can we predict earthquakes? I wanted to help solve these challenges.

My early career in metals exploration was exciting and I relished almost every minute. Even in my free time, I continued to study ore deposits in the literature and to examine rocks in new locations. My enjoyment of geology ruined other career options for me. Nothing else could equal the thrill of discovery or the freedom of exploration. I marveled at mist-filled sunrises, incredible waterfall landscapes, and dazzling sunsets in the high north Cascades of western Washington, the Pioneer Range of central Idaho, or the Humboldt-Toiyabe Forest of Nevada. And my close encounters with animals of all types would thrill even a seasoned wildlife photographer.

I worked very hard in my early career and was fortunate to have joined Burlington Northern during a time of growth and change in the minerals group. Within three years, I became supervisor of land and minerals and was placed in charge of the geologic appraisals for the land exchange program BN was doing with the federal government. BN owned 8.5 million acres of checkerboard-pattern land from Minnesota to Washington, the largest private land ownership in the world outside of the Soviet Union. Both BN and the federal government wanted to consolidate the land for better management of their respective ownerships, so a land-trading program was initiated.

Before the land could be exchanged, the value of all resources had to be determined so that the trades could be balanced and equal. My job was to coordinate the land appraisals by BN's timber, coal, iron ore, oil and gas, industrial minerals, geothermal, and metallic minerals groups and to determine an overall value for both the BN ownership and the federal land ownership in the exchange. During my time as supervisor of land and minerals, we exchanged more than one million acres of land, the greatest quantity of land ever exchanged with the federal government in our nation's history. As supervisor, I learned how to value resources and to work with and manage people.

Sometimes our fieldwork in the land evaluation program was extremely difficult. In order to be a good leader when the most difficult jobs were at hand, I usually would go to the field. One of our most challenging areas to work was an isolated area of Burlington Northern lands running along the upper St. Joe River in northern Idaho. The mountains in this area were quite steep, the vegetation thick, and the road access almost nonexistent. Both black bears and grizzlies densely populated the upper St. Joe lands. Although they were young, physically fit, and adept at traveling in the forest, my crews of four geologists had not been able to take the necessary stream sediment samples.

We decided that if we didn't want to spend the night in the bear-infested forest, we must take advantage of the long hours in mid-June and work a couple of very long days. We set our alarms for 2:30 a.m. so we could shower, dress, and drive the two-hour-long dirt road to the place where we would park our trucks. As dawn was breaking at 5:00 a.m., we were falling down waterfalls and slick brush to our destination in the St. Joe River. Along the way we heard bear moving on the hillside, we smelled the presence of bear, and we saw bear scat and bear-marked trees. But thankfully we didn't actually visually encounter any. By 7:00 a.m. we were wading in the river rapids and taking sediment samples as we traveled. There were no trails along the river, not even game trails. The combination of fast-moving water, downed wet timber, and slick rocks made walking difficult and dangerous. We managed to travel about four miles by our noon break, sampling along the way. We gobbled our sandwiches and water in just a few minutes and we continued along the river. Whenever we intersected a creek coming into the river, we sampled that, as well. We continued for another four miles and we were exhausted. At 7:00 p.m. when we started our ascent to the waiting trucks, it was all we could do to slowly pull ourselves and our packs up the steep mountainside. We could only make it up ten to fifteen feet before we had to rest our aching bodies. We said to each other, "If we see a bear, we are too exhausted to run and we will have to just let him eat us." Very slowly we progressed up the mountainside, and at 10:00 p.m., we finally reached the dirt road back to our pickups. We used head lamps to follow the road and we arrived at our trucks about 11:00 p.m. Our samples were loaded and we drove the dark roads back to our motel. We saw deer, elk, and even a bear in the headlights. We arrived completely exhausted at the motel at 1:30 a.m. Two days later we repeated the long day sampling on another section of the upper St. Joe.

Another difficult area in which to work was the Burlington Northern land along the western slopes of the Cascade Mountain Range in Washington. Often we had to use machetes to carve a path through the thick vegetation, and the terrain was the steepest we ever worked. One time we literally spent the entire day falling down waterfalls. We would take just one step forward and then we fell for about twenty directly down the slick hillside. The vegetation hopefully slowed our fall, and we grabbed vines and limbs on our descent. Then we would take another step and fall again. Along the way we would map any outcrops and take rock samples.

Doug was working with me and he had shredded his Levis on the rocks and brush. There was a large hole near one knee and a second large hole near his crotch. Because the vegetation was so thick, we sometimes didn't see blind holes that caused us to fall down the mountainside. Suddenly Doug disappeared into one of these blind holes. Then I heard a hair-raising scream. I scrambled over to see what had happened. Doug had fallen about thirty feet down the mountain. To make matters worse, he had straddled a tall devil's club plant for the last fifteen feet. As he slid down the devil's club, thousands of sharp barbs were thrust into his bare leg and crotch area. He was in agony, and so I helped him up and we made a plan to work our way back to our truck as quickly as possible. The next evening, we laughed about the event over beers.

As our land exchange program began to wind down, my job and responsibilities at Burlington Northern changed. Our coal and minerals subsidiary company was separated from Burlington Northern Inc. and renamed Meridian Minerals Company. My title changed to chief geologist, metals at Meridian Minerals Company. As a result of the spike in gold prices in late 1979 and early 1980, I was allowed to change my responsibilities from evaluating the metallic minerals on company lands to exploring for and discovering new gold deposits in the western United States. This change worked in my favor because, as a geologist, I loved gold exploration the most.

Following the gold price spike, Meridian Minerals Company opened new offices in Spokane, Washington, and Reno, Nevada, and soon I had a total of twenty geologists and support staff who worked for me. I managed a $2 million-per-year exploration program working in Washington, Idaho, Montana, Oregon, California, Nevada, Utah, and Arizona.

Within a few years, things again changed at Meridian. In 1983, gold prices had fallen below $400 per ounce, and our BN parent company executives in Minneapolis decided that maybe Meridian should exit the gold exploration business. So Bruce Ennis, then the CEO of Meridian, met with me and said that in a year there would be a meeting to decide whether BN would stay in gold exploration. In the interim, I would have complete freedom to evaluate the business and to formulate an argument as to why BN should remain. Our metals exploration group had permission to interview anyone, to travel anywhere, to bring people to Billings, and to do whatever was needed to gain an understanding of the business. This was a tremendous opportunity. Even if BN chose to not stay in the gold exploration business, I could drastically expand my knowledge within a year and then "write my own ticket" as far as future employment was concerned.

The managers I interviewed were impressively honest and forthcoming with information. We also interviewed consulting geologists and asked them how they thought various companies could improve and be more successful. We compiled a chart of total exploration expenditures versus the dollar value of exploration success for each company. Then we focused on what the best companies were doing right. As our study continued, my list of contacts and friends in the exploration business was growing exponentially.

Equipped with the necessary information, our presentation to the BN executives was well received, and we convinced the company to go forward with metals exploration, at least for the time being. However, BN had decided ultimately to focus only on the railroad industry and to either sell or close all its subsidiaries, including Meridian.

During the last year of my tenure at Meridian, I hired a gentleman who was regarded as the world's leading expert on both volcanogenic massive sulfide deposits and submarine exhalite gold deposits. These submarine exhalites were known to be hosted in the Archean-aged greenstones of Ontario, Canada. After attending a symposium on gold deposits in Canada, I suspected that the majority of the gold deposits I had examined on the Main and West Belts of the Mother Lode Gold District of California were also these metamorphically remobilized, submarine exhalites.

My expert geologist gladly accepted my invitation to teach in Billings for two days and then travel with us on our company jet to California and view these deposits in the field. Soon, we were in the field viewing the rocks of the Mother Lode. We had a great trip home on the company jet complete with fresh seafood, which the pilots had picked up in San Francisco.

As soon as I returned to Billings, I grabbed our land man, and the two of us flew back to California to meet with the property owner of the West Belt deposit I had identified on the field trip. The property owner was a former marine colonel who was then engaged in turkey farming. We were able to persuade him to sign a reasonable lease agreement. We began exploration on his property and our efforts eventually led to the delineation of a medium-sized (700,000-ounce) gold deposit, which we named the Royal Mountain King after the former underground mine on the property. I received a bonus of $8,000 from Meridian for finding this deposit. Meridian's profit from three years of mining was more than $200 million.

For many other gold companies in the 1980s and 1990s, exploration success became the kiss of death for the exploration staff. As soon as a proven discovery was made, the foolish companies would deem the exploration staff no longer necessary and fire them. Success at Meridian was the kiss of death for gold exploration, as well.

After I left Meridian, I decided to start my own exploration company, Cavanaugh Minerals. My idea was to acquire gold exploration properties via claim staking and then lease those properties to major mining companies for exploration. My real profit would come from a retained royalty in each property. My mother was steadfastly opposed to my going into business for myself. She was certain I would fail. In the beginning, she was right.

Cavanaugh Minerals existed for one year before I realized that the properties I had acquired in Idaho, Montana, and Oregon were too small to be of interest to a major mining company. It was foolish for me to acquire such small properties, the largest of which was only eight claims (or 160 acres) in size. I knew from experience that properties had to be larger to interest major mining companies, but because we had very little savings, I didn't have the money to stake larger claim blocks. During that year, I used up most of our savings anyway and Cavanaugh Minerals ended up being a bust. Although Cavanaugh Minerals did not succeed, I loved what I was doing and I worked very hard. My goal was to learn from my experiences and acquire properties of sufficient size and quality to interest major exploration companies in the future.

# CHAPTER EIGHT: ECM, INC.

In early 1986, I received a telephone call from Bruce Ennis. Bruce had been the CEO of both Meridian and Montco Coal Company. He had practiced business law in Montana and had taught law at the University of Montana. Bruce asked about my current activities and I told him I was acquiring gold properties via Cavanaugh Minerals, but I was looking for an investment so I could acquire larger properties. He said we should discuss the possibility of working together, first in a grubstake arrangement and later to build an exploration company. Under the grubstake arrangement (as was the historical tradition in the gold exploration business), Bruce would provide a monetary investment in return for a share of the profits in whatever I discovered.

We met for the first time outside of Meridian later that week. Bruce said that before he could invest in me, he had to understand the strength of my exploration ideas. He wanted a list of prospective properties that we could acquire and a short description of the opportunity for each property. I selected twenty properties in Washington and twenty properties in Nevada as potential targets for acquisition. On that list, my second highest ranked target in Nevada was the property that hosted the twenty-plus million-ounce Pipeline gold deposit. One of my Washington targets was the Magnetic property, which included the Buckhorn mine where a one million-ounce gold deposit was later discovered.

After reviewing my list, Bruce wisely decided that we should skip the grubstake and just form a company and work together. Bruce would invest $30,000 in the company and I would invest $15,000 (which was all the money I had remaining in my bank account). From the $45,000 total, I would be paid a salary of $2,000 per month to keep my family alive, and we would use the remaining $21,000 in the first year to explore and then acquire larger properties.

Once we had a few good acquisitions, the plan was to raise additional capital from outside investors. The company would be named ECM, Inc., using the initials for Ennis Cavanaugh Minerals, Incorporated. Bruce would own two-thirds of the company and I would own one-third in proportion to our initial investments. Bruce would act as vice president and secretary of the company and I would serve as president and treasurer of ECM, Inc.

During the first year of ECM, we spent $6,000 on travel costs, sampling shipment costs, and geochemical analyses. By the fall of 1986, we had only $15,000 remaining in our treasury and we owned only two rather anemic properties, one in Montana and one in Washington. Bruce and I agreed that it was critical that we acquire at least one more property in "elephant country" in order to make ourselves more attractive to outside investors. So I told him our best opportunity was to acquire the property we had identified in the Crescent Valley of Lander County, Nevada, near the old mining camp of Gold Acres. We would call it Gold Acres South, or the GAS property. To have the first one hundred claims located and recorded professionally would cost us $150 per claim, or all of our remaining treasury. We would be betting our entire company—and perhaps our future—on this one property. But we recognized that we really had no choice, so we made the decision to take the risk and stake the property.

In the fall of 1986, we contracted with a professional claim staking company headquartered in Missoula, Montana, to do our claim staking work. After our crew arrived in the field, they telephoned us late one night with bad news. Another competing staking crew was finishing up in the same area to the north. It turned out that Goldfields Mining Company had targeted almost the same property that I had targeted. But Goldfields stopped claim staking at the topographic map boundary, so we were able to stake the southern 50 percent of our target location. In the next two months, we borrowed money to add another one hundred claims to expand the ownership block to two hundred claims covering four thousand acres, or about six square miles.

In April 1987, I attended a symposium entitled Bulk Mineable Precious Metal Deposits of the Western United States held at John Ascuaga's Nugget in Sparks, Nevada. During that symposium, I presented my geologic summary of the Gold Acres South property to exploration managers of twenty-two different companies. Yet none of the major exploration companies was interested in making a lease agreement with ECM. Many exploration managers told me in detail why they thought the property had no exploration potential for gold. Most thought that the alluvium, or water-transported soil and gravel cover, over the rocks in the Crescent Valley was too deep to drill through. I was discouraged that my selling abilities were not adequate in this first attempt, but I believed that the property was a first-class gold exploration property.

Finally, I presented the project to Stan Dempsey, the president of Royal Gold Inc. and Bruce's friend. Stan said that he might be interested in a deal if, after completing a field evaluation, his consulting geologist recommended the property for acquisition. Stan hired Dick Thompson to do the field evaluation. Dick was an old friend of mine and a fair geologist who would make a decision based on the facts in the field. I met Dick in the Crescent Valley and together we toured the old Gold Acres mine site. I showed Dick the results of the USGS sampling, which indicated that there was a gold and pathfinder element anomaly extending to the southeast from Gold Acres under the alluvial cover. Pathfinder elements, such as arsenic, antimony, and mercury, travel farther in the auriferous hydrothermal fluids, and their detection in rock samples provides information on the direction to the gold mineralization. The rocks under the cover were Paleozoic-aged, silty limestones: the right host rocks. Dick's concern was that the alluvium was too deep, as indicated by the gravity data published by the USGS. I told him that the valleys of Nevada were faulted on one side and hinged on the other. The resultant displacement along the faulted side might be thousands of feet, but the displacement on the hinged side might be very gradual and only a few tens of feet. The Crescent Valley is faulted on the southeast margin, so our side, the northwest side, should be the hinged side. We observed some prospect pits on the northwest side of the valley and we could see that the bedrock was only about ten feet below the surface of the alluvium. This observation made all the difference to Dick, and he decided to recommend the property to Royal Gold for acquisition. Very soon after, we made a lease agreement with Royal Gold, who made an additional joint venture agreement with Placer Dome.

In late 1987, ECM obtained additional funding for its exploration programs via the creation of the ECM Limited Partnership. ECM became the general partner of the partnership and the Rice family plus two geologists, Tom and Doug, became the special limited partners. The Rices agreed to finance the ECM Limited Partnership for three years at the rate of $150,000 per year. ECM's business plan was to acquire twenty properties, lease each of them to a major mining company, and retain a royalty interest. Our goal was to discover a 500,000-ounce gold deposit on one of our properties.

It was a pleasure to work with Tom, Doug, and our consulting geologist, Gordon. They were all good friends and we had many adventures together while we were exploring for gold. One day we were evaluating the Singheiser Mine in Lemhi County, Idaho, as a potential target for acquisition. I arranged to meet Doug about one mile from the mine, and we camped in separate tents on Arastra Creek that night. I enjoyed camping with Doug. We had a nice fire, cooked some hot dogs, and enjoyed several beers together. We enjoyed telling stories about our exploration adventures during the prior several weeks. About ten p.m., we settled into our sleeping bags for a good night's rest.

The air was crisp and clear the next morning and we shared a pot of coffee and some donuts. About eight a.m., we packed our packs with sample bags, holstered our rock hammers, and headed for the mine to systematically take rock samples. Doug had already spent a few days at the Singheiser developing detailed geologic maps of both the surface and underground rocks. Although the Singheiser was discovered in 1866, most of the mine production came in the 1930s. We were taking chip samples from the back and floor of the underground workings at fixed intervals to determine if the remaining gold and silver ore could be profitably mined.

Suddenly we heard noises coming from the mine entrance. We walked outside to find two wardens from the Idaho Fish and Game Department. They both had their hands on their holstered pistol grips as they approached the mine portal. They aggressively shouted to us, "What are you two doing?" We answered, "Taking rock samples. What are you doing?" We learned that these two Sherlock Holmes-quality detectives had been given an anonymous tip that there was a poached elk carcass in the Singheiser Mine. They had camped for two days on the ridge across from the mine and had watched us at our camp all evening. When we went to the mine in the morning, they had hoped to catch us red-handed with the shot-out-of-season elk. Fortunately, there were no elk in the mine workings and the game wardens were embarrassed to realize that they had staked out the mine for two days for nothing. I was embarrassed for the citizens of Idaho who paid their salaries.

While working with Tom along the west belt of the Mother Lode, I had another surprise. We were evaluating old mine workings for their gold potential. The day in central California was so hot and dry that grasshoppers would land on my bare arms and legs and try to suck up my sweat. Any liquid might help them live another day or two.

After an hour of walking, we approached an old, obscure, mine opening that probably had not been visited by humans in decades. It was located in a thick grove of poison oak along a shady creek valley. As we slowly gloved our way through the poison oak, being careful not to touch the plants more than necessary, I noticed that there was a very thick coating of brown moss on the rock surface on all sides of the opening. The brown moss looked very strange. As we arrived just a few feet from the moss, Tom said to me, "That is not moss!" He threw a pebble onto the moss and suddenly it started moving. The moss was composed of tens of thousands of spiders! Apparently they had congregated on the cold rock surface to escape the heat. After scaring most of the spiders from the mine entrance with sticks, we went in and took samples. The remaining small quantity of gold was not of interest to us, but the multitude of spiders punctuated our dreams for days. We certainly were on alert for more at each mine entrance.

In the National Mining District of Nevada, Tom and I were investigating the gold potential of a number of old mines. We had taken several mine safety courses and were well aware of the many dangers in old mine workings. Like most days of Nevada gold exploration, there was not another human within fifty miles of where we were working. We were especially aware of rattlesnakes because we had already met two in the tunnels of two other mines. On the top of the hill we knew there was a deep and sloping shaft from the 1890s. We wanted to test and sample the rocks near this shaft.

Tom trudged ahead of me up the hill toward the shaft. Before I could remind him about the possibility of a snake in the rock rubble near the mineshaft, he got down on his knees and peered into the shaft. There was a whishing sound and Tom flew backwards as if propelled by some unseen force. At the same time he shouted, "Whaaaaaaaa?" My first thoughts were that he had peered into the face of a snake, or perhaps a bear was coming out of hibernation in the shaft! I learned later that he didn't really know what had happened because his brain didn't have time to process the information. His body just reacted to the presence of a very large, living creature coming rapidly out of the shaft. Thankfully, the animal was only a huge owl with outstretched wings! In an instant the owl was within of few feet of Tom's face. Tom was able to laugh about the experience over beers that evening.

Bruce's talents were a perfect complement to my talents. His strengths of raising money, taking care of the day-to-day business, and dealing with business legalities were in stark contrast to my strengths of managing geologists, selling properties, and conducting the geologic exploration. Although sometimes we had our disagreements, both Bruce and I loved what we were doing. Our fondness for the work was the principal reason we were so successful. Still, the business was a struggle, and we nearly ran out of capital for payroll so many times that I became accustomed to scrambling to sell a property at the last minute.

During the five-year period from 1986 through 1991, ECM, Inc. was extremely successful by any measurement. Our company set many records in the gold exploration business, records that likely will never be broken. ECM acquired a total of fifty properties covering more than 100,000 acres (more than 156 square miles). ECM acquired and held properties in Arizona, California, Idaho, Montana, Nevada, Oregon, and Washington and received more than $1.5 million in annual payments, advance minimum royalties, and bonuses for leasing its properties. A total of thirty-two different mining and exploration companies signed fifty lease agreements to explore ECM's properties. These companies spent more than $50 million in direct exploration costs on ECM's properties. In the end, three large gold deposits were discovered on ECM's Gold Acres South property. More than 5.6 million ounces of gold have been produced from this property to date and a minimum of an additional 3.5 million ounces of ore remain on ECM's land.

Patrick Cavanaugh in front of the South Pipeline Pit in Lander County, Nevada

Near the tire of a haul truck at Barrick Gold's South Pipeline gold deposit.
Left to Right: Greg Ennis (son of Bruce Ennis), Rob Palmer (husband of Alisha Cavanaugh), Patrick Cavanaugh, and Kim Cavanaugh.

I am so very fortunate to have had a career as an exploration geologist. If I lived my life over, I would choose the same career. I still love everything about being a geologist. I love the outdoors and studying natural processes. I love the challenge of trying to find something that nobody else has discovered. I love the variety involved in geologic work—the research, the thinking, the planning, the property acquisition, the exploration, and the moment of discovery. For me, geology was play. There are many thousands of locations that I likely was the first human to walk. Often I was working alone with no other humans within a fifty-mile radius. I had no cell phone, no radio, no backup if help were needed. I was alone and in pure bliss! Doing geologic exploration was so much better than working for a living.

# CHAPTER NINE: CHARACTERS, MAVERICKS, AND NUTS

One of the many things I loved about being an exploration geologist was the many unique entrepreneurs, prospectors, and characters whom I met both in remote mountain locations and in some not-so-remote locations. Some of these larger-than-life rebels chose to live both literally and figuratively as far from the "maddening crowd" as they could get. I was also fortunate to meet some of the legends of the era who lived and worked in cities. I tried to learn a little about myself from these special characters.

In the Sweet Grass Hills of Montana, I met "Cowboy Jake" (obviously not his real name). Jake, a man who was born a cowboy, raised a cowboy, and would always be a cowboy, was born on a ranch in Wyoming. Jake lived in a tarpaper shack in a very remote part of the Sweet Grass Hills, which are three large mounds that stick up out of the north central Montana prairie. If they were located in the Midwest or Eastern United States, they would probably be called the Sweet Grass Mountains because they rise more than three thousand feet out of the prairie. They are covered with deep native grasses and wildflowers at the lower elevations and with fir, pine, and aspen on the upper elevations. The Sweet Grass Hills are pristine and untouched, and I suspect they appear today just as they were when the first humans in North America saw them. In my estimation, wild game is more abundant in the Sweet Grass Hills than in any other place in the United States. Innumerable deer, elk, antelope, foxes, coyotes, badgers, skunks, porcupines, marmots, ground squirrels, pheasant, grouse, partridges, turkeys, and other animals frolic on the flanks of the hills. If you visit any of the Sweet Grass Hills, the abundance of wildlife will thrill you.

I didn't believe that real cowboys still existed in the 1980s, but Jake certainly looked like one. He wore old, stained clothing, including chaps, a vest, a bandana, and a large-brimmed cowboy hat that had seen decades of use. His old dusty boots sported a few holes and rusty spurs on the back. His sun-beaten skin was testament to a full life lived in the outdoors. He had no running water, no electricity, and very little food other than coffee, jerky, beans, and beer. Jake owned two horses and a small herd of cattle. He spoke very slowly in a low voice (almost a whisper) that told you he had spent many years in the saddle alone. Jake owned a small parcel of land that gave access to Gold Hill, the largest central hill in the Sweet Grass Hills. He said it would be fine to cross his land, but said, "You won't find what you're lookin' for out there." Later I had my samples analyzed I found out he was right—there were only very tiny traces of gold in the Sweet Grass Hills.

When I sat and visited with Jake, I envied his simple lifestyle. He didn't need much human contact because he had his Western novels, his dog, and his horses for company. He did not have any radio or television and really did not care. He couldn't have told you much about current events, not even what happened within the last decade. But he did have some simple wisdom and humor that made him very likeable. He let me take his picture, and I look at it occasionally to remember this real-life cowboy. From Jake I learned that there is some cowboy in all of us who long for the solitude of wilderness.

I met Howard (also not his real name) in the Tobacco Root Mountains of Montana in the late 1980s. Howard was a true maverick (in fact, that moniker was etched on his tombstone when he died in 1995). His claim to fame was that he had invented a televiewer, a forerunner to the VCR. Howard staked the first mining claims on uranium in the Wyoming Gas Hills and went on to form a number of uranium mining companies, such as Western Standard Uranium Corporation. With the money he earned in the uranium fields, he moved to rural southwestern Montana and invested in auto dealerships. In Montana, Howard owned Packard, Hudson, and Chevrolet dealerships and the Ennis, Montana, newspaper.

To say that Howard was a character was an understatement—he was a character's character. Howard learned to purchase patented mining claims when they went up for sale for back taxes. Often he would be the only buyer when the properties went up for sale on the county courthouse steps, so he obtained the properties for payments ranging from $10 to $500. Over the years, Howard had amassed a large percentage of the patented mining claim properties in southwestern Montana using very little capital.

Using his "self-taught mining skills," Howard had attempted to mine several of his properties. He failed miserably and made a series of environmental messes in the process. Later, he became involved in a long series of lawsuits over water rights when he claimed title to "all of the surface and underground water in the Jefferson River Valley" as a result of his ownership of the patented mining claims. The litigation with nearby ranchers continued for years and exhausted almost all of his remaining resources. This did not quench his unrelenting optimism about all of his properties.

He billed himself to several Montana newspapers as the "richest man in the world" by his calculations. Shockingly, several newspapers did publish his press releases that indicated he had discovered the largest platinum deposits in the United States. One issue of the *Spokane Chronicle* stated that according to Howard, "His company is looking for help to develop three or four world-class platinum and gold deposits . . . hosting more than 100 million tons of ore." Howard goes on to say in the article that "three thousand jobs or more will eventually be created in Madison County through the discoveries, and thus Madison County has the best economic future of the fifty-six counties in Montana." Howard claimed to have spent seven years and $2 million developing his patented mining claims. It is certain that he spent seven years.

When I met Howard, he drove an old rusted Chevy Suburban. This was perhaps the only remnant of his prior car dealerships. He wore a ragged shirt and overalls and sported an old stained cowboy hat that had endured many Montana winters. Yet he walked erect and confident. He truly believed in his properties and he truly believed he was the "richest man in the world."

Over the course of a week, I visited all of Howard's properties in the field with him as my "tour guide." Despite my experience with other optimistic prospectors, it was amazing to watch how he could convince himself that there was value where there clearly was none. I was interested in his gold properties, but he tried to steer me to his platinum properties, which he believed to be huge. The gold properties had once contained some gold, but the remaining gold mining potential was very limited. The platinum properties were large, but the results of my sampling confirmed that there was no platinum (or platinum group metals) anywhere within them. Like many other prospectors, Howard did not believe me when I told him his properties had no value. Unlike most other prospectors, however, Howard lived in a real fantasy world. He believed his properties had a gross value of more than $100 billion. He was insulted because "I was just like all the other foolish geologists who could not recognize the obvious gold and platinum values even when they were right before my eyes." I told Howard that it was a pleasure to meet him and we both said goodbye after our two weeks together. From Howard I learned that sometimes there should be a limit to our optimism.

It was the Kettle River Mountain Range in eastern Washington where I met Lee (again not his real name). I was investigating a gold prospect for Meridian on the margin of the range in an area of mixed ownership of BN and National Forest lands. Because the area was far from existing roads, I was using my small Honda 150 motorcycle for transportation. As I drove the Honda up to the prospect, I was bothered by the persistent sensation that someone was watching me.

The work took all morning to complete. The sun was high in the sky by the time I collected rock samples all over the area, bagged and labeled them, and put them in my backpack. As I was heading back down the trail, suddenly a man appeared to the side, just standing there watching me. He was tall, muscular, and bald headed. A very large growth protruded from the top of his head. It was difficult for me to remain calm and not recoil upon seeing this grotesque-looking man.

I said hello. The stranger said hello back and then he muttered, "I have been watching you all morning." "Oh," I said, "well, I was just about to have some lunch. Do you want to join me? I have plenty." He hesitated and then replied, "Oh . . . okay." We sat down and I shared a couple sandwiches, two apples, some chips, and a couple bottles of water. We talked as we ate, and I learned that he lived in a small mobile home just a few miles up the valley.

He asked what I was doing with the motorcycle and I told him I was evaluating the gold potential of the old prospect. He said, "I guess that is okay." He said that he owned some private land himself "nearby." He smiled broadly, revealing a few missing teeth, as he told me that when he first saw me, "I almost shot you, but decided not to at the last minute." I sort of brushed that off as idle talk until I learned that he had a large crop of marijuana growing not far away. He said he grew it for medical purposes. He thought I was "with the government" and he did not like "government men." I reiterated that I was just out on my own doing some prospecting. That made him comfortable and we had a good long chat.

Lee made his living by growing a garden, hunting in the area, and cultivating a little weed. He seldom saw anybody in this remote valley and was eager to talk. Over the next several hours, he told me his life story. He had lived a difficult life and had spent some time in prison "a few years back."

Lee was very friendly to me and told me I could come back anytime. I was glad we had become friends. As we departed, he showed me the nickel-plated .38-caliber pistol he kept in his back pocket. "I use it on government men," he said coolly. I was happy he decided not to shoot me. From Lee I learned that with kindness, I could overcome fear.

While I was working for Meridian in the southernmost Sierra Nevada mountain range of California, east of Bakersfield, I met Dale (not his real name). Dale drove a brand new Cadillac, but he lived in an old trailer house near the ghost town of Loraine, California. Dale was a large man with a firm handshake. I first contacted Dale because I wanted to evaluate his property, the Old Cowboy Mine, a silver and gold deposit that I thought might still contain some significant ore. Past production had centered on a wide, dip-slope vein that might be amenable to open pit mining. If my samples came back with sufficient silver values, I might want to make a deal with Dale that would ultimately make him a millionaire.

But this simple old prospector had already been a millionaire, twice.

At first, I was skeptical of his stories, but he showed me pictures and memorabilia that proved they were true. He had made his first million in the booming real estate market of Southern California following World War II. All that was needed in those days was a little capital to purchase the first apartment house. Using several years worth of rental income and his credit he bought more apartments. Eventually, Dale had accumulated properties worth several millions of dollars. He sold those properties and invested in a wholesale business. But within a few years, Dale lost all his money in the business.

In the spirit of dogged resilience that many of these men embodied, Dale reinvented himself as an inventor. He invented a process for spraying on a waterproof coating beneath the shingles on roofs. A roofing manufacturing company paid Dale $2 million for the patent on the spraying process. Dale proudly showed me a photo of the check being presented by executives of the roofing company. Dale then told me, "I spent it all on women and booze."

My rock samples showed that the remaining silver in the mine was not quite economically viable. This was not a surprise to Dale, who had purchased the property for other reasons. He recognized that the schistose sediments hosting the Cowboy Mine had been hydrothermally altered to some rare clay minerals. These clay minerals could be used in the porcelain industry because they were very pure and because the deposit was located less than one hundred miles from the population center of Los Angeles. He was already working on plans to joint venture with a clay company and make his third million. Dale told me that once you know you have the ability to make large sums of money, it becomes much easier to do. From Dale, I learned that confidence and persistence pays, repeatedly.

In the northern Sierras near the town of Nevada City, California, I met a man I will call the "unknown soldier." I had been evaluating a series of gold deposits in the region that may have still contained large ore reserves. Most of the gold deposits were high-temperature hydrothermal veins that could be very high grade but small in size. I was searching for a swarm of these veins that could be mined in bulk, either from the surface or underground.

I don't remember my exact location, just that I had been traveling on dirt roads most of the day and had driven very far into the Tahoe National Forest. At the end of the day, I was traveling on a little used, single-track road, a road so rugged I was plowing down small, foot-high pine trees with my Chevy pickup. At several locations, I passed "no trespassing" signs, a common sight in many national forests and on BLM-administered federal lands. I had passed hundreds of such signs in my career as an explorationist. Many people, such as hunters, berry pickers, ranchers, and prospectors, put them up to keep others from entering. I frequently voiced my frustration with the lack of penalty for putting up such a sign on public lands.

The summertime air in the Sierra Nevada forest was invigorating and rich in oxygen. My window was down and I was enjoying my solitary drive. All of a sudden, I heard someone shrieking. As soon as I stopped my truck, a man jumped down from the heavily timbered mountainside. He was wearing camouflaged army fatigues and his face was painted in camouflaged colors. Around his waist was a belt on which several grenades hung menacingly. More importantly, he held an assault rifle that was pointed directly at my head. "Turn around and go back, you *#@&*!" I only hesitated a second before throwing the truck in reverse. As I backed up, the "unknown soldier" ran toward me. I increased my speed backwards, and when I rounded the corner, he was gone from view. I continued backing rapidly for about half a mile until there was room to turn around.

Now really ready to call it a day, I went back to the motel in Nevada City and ate a good dinner at the local restaurant. I learned from the waitress that there were many marijuana operations in the area and some people were very aggressive about protecting their grow plots. I made a mental note to not venture into that area again. The unknown soldier taught me to pay closer attention to signs.

While working in the Panamint Range of California in 1982, I met Dorsey Wingo, the director of operations and chief pilot for the Rialto, California, based Western Helicopters. Meridian Mineral Company needed extensive helicopter support for our exploration program in the Panamint Mountain Range. Most of the range is very steep and I decided we would save both time and money by using helicopters for transport during about two weeks of rock sampling and geological mapping. The Panamint Range is located just west of Death Valley and has many gold deposits and an old mining ghost town named Ballarat on the western side. In the south end of the mountain range up the Goler Wash road is the Barker Ranch, where the Charles Manson family lived and was finally arrested. There are numerous survivalist camps within the old gold workings in the Panamint Range.

Flying in the Panamint Range is more dangerous than normal helicopter work. The steepness of the range combined with the high air temperatures and risks from nearby military traffic make this some of the most perilous flying in the United States. Noranda Mining and Exploration had crashed one helicopter in the Panamint Range about five years before, killing two or three geologists and seriously injuring several others. I had friends that survived that crash. A large number of small airplanes of various types have crashed in the Panamint Mountains during the last twenty-five years.

Nevertheless, we all felt very safe flying with Dorsey in the Panamints. Dorsey had been flying helicopters for about thirteen years (since Vietnam where he earned his Purple Heart). He was exceedingly careful as a pilot and took every precaution. Before he began each flight, he reviewed safety procedures with everyone in great detail. As we spent more time with Dorsey, we got to know him well and we learned about his recent experiences as a pilot.

Just a few months before our time in the Panamints, Dorsey Wingo was piloting a chopper used for the filming of the *Twilight Zone* movie. On July 23, 1982, his olive drab UH-1B Huey helicopter fell out of the sky and decapitated actor Vic Morrow and a Vietnamese girl. A second Vietnamese girl was crushed by the falling helicopter. The National Transportation Safety Board (NTSB) attributed the crash to "the detonation of debris-laden high-temperature special effects explosions too near a low-flying helicopter, leading to foreign object damage to one rotor blade and delamination due to heat to the other rotor blade, the separation of the helicopter's tail rotor assembly, and the uncontrolled descent of the helicopter." Dorsey was able to control the crash of the helicopter sufficiently to save all the people on board the aircraft. He spent enough time with us to tell his version of the accident before there was a hearing or any lawyers involved. It was a very painful story for him to tell.

After the accident, the combination of NTSB hearing, pretrial hearing, and the trial itself occupied six years of Dorsey's life. After being cleared by the jury, Dorsey began helicopter logging, which he continued for the next two decades. Dorsey has been called the Mark Twain of helicopter pilots and has written two books about his experiences. From Dorsey, I learned that just as Clint Eastwood said in the movie *Unforgiven*, "It's a hell of a thing, killing a man" (to say nothing of killing two young girls too).

I feel very fortunate to have known Maxie Anderson while I was working for Meridian in the early 1980s. We traveled to Albuquerque, New Mexico, on BN's corporate jet (a Westwind II) to meet with Maxie at the headquarters of his company, Ranchers Exploration. His headquarters building was a showcase office complex for its time, boasting 19,500 feet of office space in three buildings, a 5,000-square foot spa, a childcare facility, and a full-size racquetball court, all contained on five acres of exquisitely landscaped property.

Maxie Anderson was an extremely innovative entrepreneur and balloonist. He graduated with a degree in industrial engineering from the University of North Dakota at age twenty-eight. The following year he was appointed to the board of directors of Ranchers Exploration, and six years later he was made president and CEO of the firm. Ranchers was at first a uranium royalty company, which under Maxie became one of the most forward-thinking mining companies in the industry.

Maxie's creative ideas and courage led to the first commercial development of copper dump leaching, followed by solvent extraction-electrowinning of cathode copper (SX-EW). This Ranchers Exploration-pioneered technology became the standard for many copper mining operations throughout the world. After their success with SX-EW, Ranchers purchased the Big Mike Mine and rapidly mined direct shipping ore that went to foreign smelters. At another Arizona mine, Ranchers Exploration exploded the largest non-nuclear blast of all time and then leached the copper in situ for the first time ever. In all of these creative ventures, Ranchers Exploration garnered huge profits.

Always looking for the better way, Maxie was creative in his business practices, as well. He loved joint ventures and created many of them with companies from all over the world. He initiated profit sharing, employee empowerment activities, hedging techniques, and innovative financing techniques. He paid dividends in gold and silver bars and he financed new mines with borrowed bullion. He pioneered innovative business practices for many industries.

Maxie had been a pilot from age fifteen, and he was a world-class balloonist who was inducted into the US Ballooning Hall of Fame. He was one of three balloonists to first cross the Atlantic Ocean in his Double Eagle II balloon in 1978. Sadly, Maxie died in a balloon crash in Germany on June 27, 1983. The following year, Hecla Mining purchased Maxie's company for $194 million.

My geologists and I had encountered Ranchers geologists in numerous locations, and we suggested that perhaps BN and Ranchers should joint venture some properties. We had extensive talks with Maxie and his executives during a two-day meeting. Our goal was to negotiate a joint venture with Ranchers Exploration so that they might have the rights to explore some of the 8.5 million acres of Burlington Northern Lands for minerals and BN might participate in some of Ranchers' other ventures. Unfortunately, we were unable to reach agreement on the terms of a deal. I was very impressed with Maxie and his accomplishments. Maxie taught me that a good leader should be open to new ideas and always puts his employees first.

In 1992, I met Nelson Bunker Hunt in the waiting room of the uppermost offices of Scotiabank in Toronto. I had traveled to Toronto on a one-day notice to meet with a group of potential investors to try to raise $2 million for our fledgling Vancouver-listed company, White Knight Resources. As the president of White Knight Resources US, I was in charge of the exploration program in Nevada. Before we could drill our properties, we had to raise the money. My one-hour presentation was key to our getting the financing. Armed with a single map and my own knowledge of Nevada gold deposits, I was about to give the presentation of my life.

Before my Vancouver-based lawyer and I went in for the presentation,

I visited with Bunker Hunt. He and several of his people were waiting for the next appointment with the same investor group with whom I was meeting. We were in effect competing for new finance dollars from the same people. Time permitted us to outline "our deal" and "his deal" in some detail. Bunker was looking to finance a new Texas offshore oil venture. He was very personable and cordial considering he was once considered the "richest man in the world."

As I went in to give my presentation, Bunker smiled and wished me luck. My presentation was well received and I handled the questions well. The investor group said they would give us the $2 million the following Monday. On my way out, Bunker Hunt asked, "Did you make the deal?" "Yes," I replied. He smiled and gave me a thumbs-up.

Bunker Hunt was one of seven children in the "first family" of H. L. Hunt, a pioneer of the Texas oil boom. At the peak of his wealth, Bunker Hunt owned five million acres of grazing land in Australia, one thousand thoroughbreds on farms from Ireland to New Zealand, offshore wells in the Philippines and Mexico, and an empire of skyscrapers, sugar companies, banks, valuable art, mining holdings, and the Shakey's Pizza restaurant chain. Before Muammar Gaddafi nationalized the Libyan oil fields, Bunker Hunt controlled eight million acres in an oil field three times the size of the East Texas field that gave birth to the Texas oil boom. He was worth between $8 and $16 billion.

After his losses in Libya, Bunker wanted to invest in something safe because he feared a worldwide financial collapse. His solution was to buy silver. The three Hunt brothers aggressively purchased silver until they had accumulated the rights to 200 million ounces. In 1980, insiders at the Comex and the Chicago Board of Trade, together with their friends at the Commodities Futures Trading Commission and the Federal Reserve Bank, panicked and passed regulations that trapped the Hunt brothers. On March 27, 1980—Silver Thursday—the price of silver fell to the point that the Hunt brothers could not meet a margin call. Bunker lost many of his billions because of the silver fall and the fall in oil and other commodities. Lawsuits, bankruptcy proceedings, massive loan payments, tax bills, and regulatory fines ate away at his fortune until in 1988, he was forced to sell 580 racehorses for $46 million. By the time I saw Bunker in 1992, he was nearly penniless.

However, he did get the money in Toronto for his oil deal in Texas. He made that deal and others pay big dividends, and seven years later, he had regained many tens of millions and returned to horse racing. I learned from Bunker Hunt to never give up—even if you lose it all.

Really successful people almost universally seem to love what they do. They excel because of their passion for their work. As a result, the Internet abounds with articles about how to "love your job." I don't agree that we should learn to love our jobs. Our affection for our work should not be forced. Instead, it should come naturally when we discover the sort of challenges that we love. As we labor with passion to solve those challenges, it is okay to make mistakes. We expect to make mistakes as part of learning how to do better. The happier we are at work, the happier we will be in all aspects of our lives.

My career continued the next several decades and so did my freedoms, my friendships, and my family life. But in the 1990s, both Susan and I stepped out of our comfort zones and began some interesting new challenges, challenges that would transform our lives forever.

# The 1990s:

## Growth Requires Leaving Your Comfort Zone

"Unless you try to do something beyond what you have
already mastered, you will never grow."

—*Ronald E. Osborn*

# CHAPTER TEN: FIRST STEPS

During our life together, Susan and I became aware of our own comfort boundaries. Although in some aspects of our lives we were brave, we knew there were many things we feared and many things that made us uncomfortable. There were many risks we would not take. We were happy living in Billings in the same home and having the same neighborhood friends. In some areas of our lives, we seldom would cross over into unfamiliar territory.

During the late 1980s and early 1990s, both Susan and I had already left our comfort zones when we each started our own businesses. As the 1990s continued, Susan and I decided to "really go for it" and we began to take more risk, to venture into terra incognita. We chose to take on the new challenges of not only being entrepreneurs, but also of public speaking, traveling, hosting exchange students, and adoption. During this decade we were also lifted into a new life of having significant wealth—this new territory would also require adaptations.

Together, Susan and I began traveling the world more and more. We also made the decision to add members to our home and family. We hosted a foreign exchange student from Chile in 1988 and another from Greenland in 1990. Our daughter, Kim, broke out of her comfort zone, too, traveling to England, Scotland, Denmark, Sweden, Finland, and the Soviet Union. As the decade ended and as our biological daughters grew older and left the nest, Susan and I decided to venture even farther beyond our comfort zone. We decided to go to Russia to adopt two children.

Meanwhile, of course, the world at large swirled around us. Things continued to change and evolve at a rapid pace. I cannot sum up the 1990s in a single characterization. It was a decade of many events: Generation X coming of age, the Persian Gulf War, the O.J. Simpson trial, *Seinfeld* on television, the rise of antigovernment militias in the United States, ethnic cleansing in the Balkans, the growth of the Internet and AOL, Princess Diana's death, the Rwandan genocide, economic globalization, the dotcom bubble, and the fear of Y2K. For me and my family, the last decade of the millennium was a time in which we left the cozy confines of the routine and the familiar, and crossed into new frontiers.

I took up speaking publicly before several large gatherings of my peers. My shyness has always made public speaking difficult. My mother was keenly aware of my shyness and she required me to take every speech class available in junior high school, high school, and college. The classes helped, but my difficulty with public speaking persisted. The night before I would have to deliver a speech, anxiety prevented me from sleeping. And when the moment came to step up to the podium, my heart would be pounding so loudly I thought everyone in the room must hear it. My whole body was bathed in sweat as I began each speech.

I had an opportunity to confront this fear when in December 1989 I spoke to a group of about nine hundred geologists as session chairman at the Northwest Mining Association meeting in Spokane, Washington. I had to say a few remarks about the session and then I had to introduce the speakers. This task was made more difficult by the fact that I didn't like one of the speakers. And yet it was a good first step for me to leave my comfort zone and stand before my peers in the mining industry and host that session. I felt very relieved afterwards.

My next public speaking "opportunity" came when I was elected American Field Service (AFS) president for Billings in 1991 and 1992. AFS was started by volunteer ambulance drivers of World Wars I and II who wanted to form an organization to promote understanding and peace among nations. It has become the leading foreign student exchange program in the United States and in the world and benefits from the work of more than eight thousand volunteers. The public speaking role of the AFS president was relatively easy because the audience always numbered one hundred or fewer people. A more challenging part of my job as AFS president was to resolve problems and disagreements between the students and their host families.

Then, in 1996, I was asked to be one of four speakers at the Workshop on the Future of the Mining Industry at the annual meeting of the American Institute of Mining, Metallurgical, and Petroleum Engineers in Santa Fe, New Mexico. This opportunity was also outside of my comfort zone. I thought about the invitation for twenty-four hours before I agreed. My nervousness motivated me to thoroughly prepare for this speech. I was surprised to learn on the day of my talk that there would be about 2,500 people in the audience. Despite the large crowd, my over-preparation helped me to speak in an entertaining fashion. Many people came up to me afterwards and complimented me on my presentation.

In 2000, the Mining and Land Resource Institute in Reno, Nevada, asked me to be the keynote speaker at their annual meeting. I reluctantly agreed. I found that I was a little less nervous this time and the audience loved my jokes. My speech was interactive and I had the audience standing and moving through much of it. Little by little, the unfamiliar, scary terrain of public speaking was becoming more navigable.

When Bruce and I staked the claims on our GAS property in Lander County, Nevada, we certainly had ventured outside our respective comfort zones. We bet our company and our futures on these few mining claims. Royal Gold began the exploration of our properties in 1988. They drilled ten holes and discovered some marginal gold mineralization, but no ore deposit. Today we know they drilled into the fringe of the Crossroads gold deposit and somehow managed to drill around the South Pipeline gold deposit without intersecting it. By the early spring of 1991, Royal Gold had spent all their money and their stock was priced at only six cents per share.

In May of 1991, Placer Dome secretly drilled a hole collared just twelve inches from the property boundary with Goldfield's claims and about 1,500 feet from our property boundary (and well within the area of influence described in our first lease/joint venture agreement). Drill hole 91-907 passed through the heart of the Pipeline deposit and intersected more than a 120-foot width of ore-grade mineralization. It was a certain discovery hole for a major

Carlin-type gold deposit! Placer Dome geologists were excited to find that two other secret holes intersected ore-grade gold, and they began to estimate the size of the massive gold ore deposit they had discovered. Bruce and I first learned of the discovery during the first week in December of 1991 at the Northwest Mining Association convention. We had dinner one evening with the vice president of exploration from Placer Dome and he told us about the drill intercept. We were overjoyed at the news! Suddenly we realized we both would likely be wealthy! Both of us would be thrust into new territory.

Gold production on ECM's claims began from a small, near surface pit (the Crescent Pit) in 1994. The South Pipeline gold deposit was defined by drilling in the 1990s, permitting was completed in 2000, and gold production began on this larger deposit in 2001. Also a portion of the GAP gold deposit and all of the Crossroads gold deposit were discovered on ECM's claims. As a result, ECM owned a small percentage gold royalty on a total of more than 9 million ounces! Gold production from ECM's property has continued from 1994 to the present.

Having wealth was well out of the comfort zone for both Susan and me. We didn't really know how to care for large sums of money and how to choose good investments. We made some mistakes along the way, but in the end we were able to diversify our assets into real estate, stocks, bonds, and annuities. Friends, family members, and even acquaintances began to treat us differently. They all wanted our help or our money. The pressure was tremendous because at first and we said yes to too many requests for monetary help. The more we said yes to loans and gifts, the more requests we received. Soon we couldn't say yes anymore. Everyone, it seemed, needed money and thought we were an easy target. Our newfound wealth had really put us into a realm beyond our comfort zone and we had to learn to say no. In addition to helping family and friends, we decided to first donate each year to nonprofit organizations helping orphans (especially in Russia). We also donated to other nonprofits helping with causes close to our hearts. We donated more than $1.5 million over the course of several years. Today we still get requests for money from family members and others. Fortunately, the monetary requests have slowed.

# CHAPTER ELEVEN: EXCHANGE STUDENTS

The decision to host a foreign exchange student was not an easy one for our family. This was a big step out of our collective comfort zone. It started when Kim had become interested in participating in the AFS program as an exchange student in her senior year. During the summer of 1987, Kim traveled with the People to People Student Ambassador Program to England, Scotland, Denmark, Sweden, Finland, and the Soviet Union. She stayed with host families in Denmark, Sweden, and England. After this experience, she wanted to have an exchange student join our family. When the opportunity arose, Susan and I debated for several days whether we really wanted to have a stranger live with us. We had learned that there would be all sorts of problems in hosting a student, but we decided to slowly face our fears and perhaps allow a foreign student to stay with us beginning in the fall of 1989.

But before then, in October of 1988, we learned that there was an AFS student from Chile who wanted to change to a new host family in Billings. Suddenly, we had to decide whether we would accept this student in our home. Together, the members of our family decided to host this needy foreign student. We knew we would have to make adjustments in our daily family life, but we decided to take a risk. As the Nike slogan goes, "Just do it."

Cristian joined our family the next day. Cristian was from an upper-middle-class family who lived in a suburb of Santiago, Chile. His father Hugo had been a regional judge in northern Chile, but during the time of Cristian's student exchange, he was working as a notary in Santiago. For the first several months of Cristian's stay in Great Falls, he lived with his assigned host family, a Korean-American family that retained many of their Korean ways of life. They ate Korean food and obeyed Korean customs. Cristian had great difficulty adapting because he had expected a "normal" American family.

AFS agreed to move Cristian to Billings and find him a new host family. We became that new host family. Over several months, Cristian became a part of our family and we treated him as a son. Cristian shared my love for fishing, and I took him on several fishing trips to the Bighorn River and to various nearby creeks and lakes. Susan and I also took him skiing and snowboarding many times. When spring came, Cristian went with our family to Yellowstone National Park. Later, we all traveled together to the biggest mall in North America, the West Edmonton Mall in Edmonton, Canada.

Everyone in our family learned a considerable amount about Chile and the Chilean culture as a result of Cristian's time with us. We learned that the most important value in that culture is family and that for Chileans, family always comes first. We also learned about the South American love of *fútbol*, or soccer, as we call it. We learned how *empanadas de mariscos* are made and about *ceviche* and *congrio frito* and other seafood dishes. We learned how to order a *completo* in Chile to get a hot dog with all the trimmings. We learned how to make a sweet syrup called *manjar blanco* by boiling a can of sweetened condensed milk. That syrup could then be used in a variety of desserts.

We also learned a great deal about our own culture and how someone from another culture viewed us. We learned how the American culture was changing and that our religious and family values were being lost. We learned about the influences of television and movies on our world view. Cristian would frequently say, "This country is going down." What this teenager meant was that the loss of family values would spell the end of the United States as a world leader.

Cristian had some interesting talents. He learned to play the guitar while staying with us, and his skills progressed nicely over the next few years. Cristian had lived in Belgium as a child, so he was fluent in French, as well as Spanish and English.

Having a new member of our family was a huge adjustment for our daughters. Kim particularly struggled with it. She had to drive Cristian to Skyview High School every day. Cristian was frequently critical of Kim and her friends. He called her a "froggy junior" while he was a senior, even though they were almost the same age. Kim was also jealous of all the attention Cristian received from her mother. In return, Cristian was jealous of both Kim and Alisha.

In spite of these challenges, it was very painful for all of our family to say goodbye to Cristian. On his final day with us, we shed many tears at the airport. Looking back now, we need not have cried. Cristian bonded so strongly with our family that he returned to visit us four times for many months each time. Both Susan and I later made trips to Chile to visit Cristian and his family, and eventually returned to Chile to attend Cristian's wedding. Our family and Cristian's Chilean family became very close for decades because of our willingness to step out of our comfort zone.

Global travel further expanded the boundaries of our comfort zone. Before the 1990s, most of our traveling was confined to the United States, Canada, and Mexico. We had traveled extensively together on camping trips in Montana and Idaho. Susan and I had flown to Hawaii twice in the 1980s and made a couple driving trips into Canada via Glacier Park. We both traveled to Mexico in our youth, and I had twice walked across the bridge from El Paso into Juarez for the day. I traveled all over the western United States as part of my career. During my twenty-five-plus years in exploration, I walked in almost every mountain range in every state in the West.

My first trip to another continent occurred in 1990, when I traveled alone to Chile to spend a week with Cristian's family and then two weeks with the Geological Association of Canada (GAC) on their field trip to many of the major mineral deposits. I was thrilled to meet the members of Cristian's family. Each one was a joy to know. Cristian's father Hugo was certainly the patriarch of the family. Together we spent a Sunday morning sitting on a park bench and speaking in French. Hugo knew that my French language skills were better than my Spanish skills. He told me all about his family and their history. He told me about the hopes and dreams he had for his children. He told me about Chile and how proud he was of his country.

I spent two days as a tourist in Santiago with Gina, Cristian's mother. Gina had a wonderful sense of humor and a high-pitched voice. When I could not understand her Spanish, her voice became a little higher. Then I really was lost, prompting a fit of congenial laughter from both of us. Little Gina, Cristian's younger sister, was a cute little girl. And Ignacio (or Nacho), Cristian's younger brother, was so much fun. Ignacio had a penchant for bargaining for good deals and he would get whatever I wanted at a big discount. His gift of gab served him well later in life.

On a trip with Hugo and Ignacio to the Chilean countryside, we passed the exact spot where President Augusto Pinochet was unsuccessfully attacked only two years before. Hugo related the details of the attack to me in French. The attackers used a bus to block the road and then advanced from the rear and sides with automatic weapons. All of Pinochet's black limos were destroyed in a hail of bullets, killing all the drivers and bodyguards, except the driver of Pinochet's limo. He executed a heroic driving maneuver and Augusto Pinochet escaped.

Hugo had just finished the story when all of a sudden a helicopter gunship appeared overhead. Within seconds, four identical black Mercedes limos zoomed by us on the highway. It was the Pinochet entourage passing at the same place where the attack on his life had occurred! I missed a great photo opportunity because Hugo insisted I not make a move for my camera while the helicopter gunships circled overhead. Although Hugo might have saved my life, I have wondered since if it just might have been possible to take that photo.

Following a wonderful week, Cristian's family dropped me at the airport, where I was to meet up with the members of the Geological Association of Canada (GAC). For thirty minutes I waited in a completely empty airport. I started to feel very uncomfortable and concerned that I had miscalculated the date when a distinguished-looking man entered the terminal. He was Colin Godwin, a professor from the University of British Columbia. I told him I was hunting for members of the GAC so I could join them on their field trip. He said he was going to do the same. I said, "There is nobody here and I am starting to worry." He asked, "Did you try the bar?" We found all forty-two other members of the GAC upstairs in the airport bar.

The field trip with the GAC was a memorable experience and one in which I made many friends, including Colin Godwin. Our field trip started in the northern Atacama Desert near Calama before heading south to visit mines and learn about the geology of the region. The Atacama Desert is the driest (non-polar) desert in the world. It is also likely the oldest desert in the world—possibly as old as 200 million years. We investigated more than 1,200 miles of mineral deposits and explored nineteen different copper, gold, silver, and iron mines in detail. We even drove our huge tour bus underground on two occasions. We stayed overnight in the Andes at two mining camps that were above 12,000 feet. A few of the mines we visited were more than 14,500 feet in elevation, and walking uphill there was a battle. My legs felt like they were made of lead as I gasped for the tiny amount of oxygen in the atmosphere.

In the Andes, we saw many vicuña, guanacos, llamas, and alpacas. We even saw "el zorro," the Chilean fox. In the Atacama Desert, we witnessed the tiny graves of hundreds of babies buried during the sodium nitrate mining boom between 1830 and 1930. We also saw full human skeletons drying in the desert sun.

We toured the largest open pit copper mine in the world, Chuquicamata. Our southernmost visit was to the world's largest underground copper mine, El Teniente, near Conception. The labyrinthine El Teniente has more than 1,900 miles of underground tunnels and drifts. As we traveled in the country, we passed through constant checkpoints where armed, stern-faced *carabineros* would ask questions and check passports. One evening at about midnight, the *carabineros* were bored and they had us unload the entire bus. Then they went through all our belongings searching for illegal fruit.

After we arrived in Santiago, we were invited to dine at the private residence of the Canadian consul, who lived in a huge mansion on a large estate in the nearby foothills. Before dinner, formally clad waiters walked around and offered trays filled with appetizers and beverages. Then we dined lavishly on empanadas, seafood, and barbequed beef, chatting throughout the evening with the consul about possible Canadian business ventures in Chile.

When I returned to the United States, Susan and I decided that we might again host an exchange student under the right circumstances. This time, we knew the challenges, so it was a little easier to step back out of our comfort zone and invite a new student into our home. In December of 1990, Ivik came to live with us. He, too, had had difficulties with his host family and needed to relocate. Some months before he left for the United States, Ivik's father had died in a helicopter crash. Ivik was no doubt traumatized by that event while simultaneously wrestling with adapting to a new culture.

Cavanaugh family in 1991. Back row: Alisha (holding Shanny), Ivik (our exchange student from Greenland holding Miki), Susan. Front row: Patrick, Duster, and Kim.

Ivik was a tall sixteen year old Greenlander with blue eyes and light brown hair. Ivik's ethnic ancestry was one-half Eskimo and one-half Danish. He was fluent in English, as well as Inuit, Danish, Swedish, Norwegian, German, and Spanish. At any given moment, he had eight or ten serious girlfriends spread throughout Greenland, Denmark, Sweden, Norway, and various cities in the United States. He seemed to have a different girlfriend "in every port," and for the most part, none of them knew about the others. Ivik was so strikingly handsome that when he went somewhere new, almost all of the women from ages sixteen to forty would turn and stare. I experienced this phenomenon when together Ivik and I entered the Billings Mustangs' baseball stadium. It was very gratifying to watch all the ladies stare, until I realized they were not staring at me.

Ivik was very much in tune with his inner self and was very comfortable being alone for long periods of time. He adored his home country of Greenland, where nature is stunningly abundant and vibrant. He shared some whale blubber with us and recounted stories of having fun on the ice and snow.

Ivik was also an excellent athlete who played on his country's national soccer team as goalie. He played soccer in Montana and quickly became famous for the distance he could kick a soccer ball (about seventy-five yards in the air). His talent earned him the kicker spot for the Skyview High School football team; in one game, he booted a sixty-yard field goal. Other players bestowed upon him the nickname "Ice" for his native environment and because he was so relaxed on the field. He showed no emotion while making a field goal under pressure. I also enjoyed playing racquetball with Ivik. He learned the sport quickly and became very skilled after a few games.

From Ivik, we learned the importance of maintaining an active lifestyle. We learned to remember to stay fit so we could enjoy all our activities to the fullest. We also learned that fully experiencing the tranquility of nature is a great blessing. Ivik affirmed what we already knew: that living in the natural world can refresh our soul.

A few years later, there were other big changes afoot. In 1993, Kim married her high school sweetheart, Steve Aita. Kim and Steve had a beautiful wedding in the Baptist church in Billings. Steve's father, Paul Aita, was the Baptist minister and officiated the ceremony. Kim looked resplendent in her wedding dress and Alisha was stunning, as well, as the maid of honor. After the wedding, Kim and Steve traveled to Oregon to attend graduate school. Kim obtained a master's degree in psychology from the University of Oregon and Steve obtained a JD degree from the Willamette University School of Law.

In 1996, we stepped out of our comfort zone in a more literal manner by moving to Boise, Idaho. It was difficult to leave our friends in Billings, but for many reasons we needed to return to Idaho. In a way we had always considered Boise as our home. For the period from 1996 through 1997 we lived in Weiser, Idaho. Susan acted as caregiver for her father, who had developed lung cancer. In Weiser, I worked as a consulting geologist. We returned to our home in Boise after Susan's father died in 1997.

Our horizons broadened a little further when, in 1997, Susan and I traveled to New Zealand, Australia, and Fiji. We spent a week in each country. In New Zealand we first stayed three days on the Coromandel Peninsula southeast of Aukland on the North Island. We loved the tropical environment on the Coromandel because it was so similar to Hawaii. I fondly remember the New Zealand sea life and the scantily clad ladies on the nude beaches. On the South Island, we stayed in Queensland. From there, we took a cruise across Lake Wakatipu, watched a sheepdog demonstration, took a jet boat ride on the Shotover River, and flew over the glacier-covered Mt. Cook. The highlight of our New Zealand trip was our cruise on the magnificent Milford Sound with its shimmering waterfalls and dancing dolphins.

In Australia, we stayed in Cairns near the Great Barrier Reef on the northeastern coast of the country. In a stroke of bad luck, Cyclone Justin arrived in Cairns just two days after our arrival. It was a Category 2 cyclone and at that time was the strongest cyclone to reach Queensland, Australia. The eye of the cyclone went directly over our hotel, which was located eighty feet from the beach. We watched from our hotel room as trees and pool furniture were tossed violently about by the powerful winds. We were also mesmerized by a small bird that held tightly to a wire as he weathered the entire storm. That bird was our hero.

In the end, Cyclone Justin killed seven people and caused more than $190 million dollars of damage. Cairns received more than thirty-nine inches of rain in a twenty-four-hour period. After the storm, we decided to go view the damage from our tiny car. We ended up being trapped in Cairns and having to get a second motel for the night because of the flooding. The Cairns Marina and boats were severely damaged; a huge storm surge had flooded everything along the coast. The waterfalls we visited after the cyclone were epic and so was the devastation on the Great Barrier Reef.

We narrowly missed Cyclone Gavin in Fiji, which took eighteen lives and devastated the outer parts of the country. When we arrived just a week after the storm, all the evidence that remained was some flooding and downed trees. In Fiji, we stayed in an inexpensive hotel not far from Suva on Viti Levu. The Fijian people are large, dark, confident, relaxed, and some of the best on earth. We got to know the maids in our hotel and we visited with several hitch-hikers whom we picked up on the road.

From behind the wheel of our rental car, we explored the island of Viti Levu. In addition to driving on the left side of the road, we were faced with the constant challenge of people and animals suddenly appearing in the narrow highway. The Fijians are accustomed to abruptly stepping out of the jungle. Fijian cows are so relaxed on the highway that they sleep there at night. It was a big surprise to come around a corner and shine the headlights on a slumbering herd sprawled across the entire pavement.

One day we had a flat tire. As soon as we pulled off the highway to repair our tire, Fijian people began to appear out of the jungle as if by magic. The men and boys took over the process of blocking the wheels, jacking the car, changing the tire, and placing the flat in the trunk. After the process, the Fijian women offered us food and beverages and then brought us soap and water to wash our hands. The natives would take nothing in return for their efforts except a thank you and a smile. We had heard before arriving that the Fijian people were considered the friendliest and kindest on earth. Our experiences confirmed this notion.

During our time in Fiji, we flew to an offshore island in a small, dilapidated Britten-Norman Islander airplane. By taking this flight, I *definitely* stepped outside my comfort zone. I watched as large, black, cumulonimbus clouds formed around Viti Levu just before our departure. As the sky grew dark, it looked as though the flight to the island would be very difficult under the best circumstances. This thunderstorm didn't look normal as it swirled in a giant black, brown, and green mushroom shape. In this old and rusty aircraft, the trip was going to be an adventure.

We took off directly into the blackest part of the storm. Within a few minutes, the tiny airplane was being thrown wildly about in the air. Our seatbelts held us in place, but loose papers and small objects flew about in the cockpit. Soon the rain came pouring into the cockpit through the leaky roof of the beat-up old plane. Nevertheless, the pilot remained calm and flew through the storm and into the sunshine. As if directed by the shining sun, we banked sharply downward and landed suddenly on a short gravel runway. I thanked God for our safe arrival.

In April 1998, Susan and I traveled to Denmark to visit Ivik and to meet some of his family. Like most tourists, we landed in Copenhagen. Ivik picked us up at the airport and we traveled to Nyborg, the Danish town where he was attending college. Ivik had a pleasant apartment in Nyborg and we felt very comfortable there.

He had to work during the weekdays, so we were on our own to explore the country. On one of our first days, we rode the train into the nearby city of Odense (pronounced OWN-sa in Danish). In Odense, we visited the Hans Christian Andersen Museum, where we learned of his life and saw his drawings and artwork. Later we visited Andersen's childhood home. On another day, Ivik drove us to Egeskov Castle, the best-preserved moat castle in Europe. The Renaissance-styled Egeskov Castle dates from 1554 and consists of two long houses connected by a thick double wall. Within the double wall are hidden stairs and a well to secure a water supply during a siege. It is truly a beautiful castle and moat pond.

We also visited the medieval Nyborg Slot (Castle) near Nyborg Town. The Nyborg castle was first completed in about 1170 and many parts were added in later centuries. In this castle, King Erik Klipping signed Denmark's first constitution in 1282. It was also the location where Denmark's first parliament met.

When we went grocery shopping in Nyborg, we had a surprise. The clerks asked us where our shopping bags were so we could carry our groceries home. We had none. We were accustomed to the United States where the question "paper or plastic?" is the norm. After some muttering about "silly Americans," we were sold a few plastic bags for about fifty cents. We carried our groceries home and discovered at the end of the week that we had very little garbage to throw in the small garbage can. There is much less waste because in Europe packaging is minimal. And the ever-present bicycles and windmills certainly made us think about how environmentally wasteful we are in the United States.

One overcast day, we decided to go on an adventure and visit some nearby old windmills and take photos. Susan and I jumped on a local bus and explained to the driver the name of the small village near the windmills. After about thirty minutes, the driver stopped the bus at an intersection and signaled to us that it was time to get off. We left the bus as instructed and it lumbered away down the highway. As soon as we looked around, we knew we were lost, surrounded in every direction by desolate, windswept farm fields.

Almost immediately, rain started coming down in horizontal sheets. We had raincoats but our pants were soon soaked. And we still had no idea which way to proceed. We decided to go up a small hill and see if we could get our bearings. There, at the top of the hill, we spotted the old windmills in the distance.

Wet but in good spirits, we trudged through the rain, which finally stopped about the time we reached the windmills. We took some lovely photos and we could see a small farm village in the distance. We walked briskly, but it took about thirty minutes to get to the village. Susan and I watched the bus drive away from the stop just as we arrived about a block away. Uh-oh.

We had no idea if or when there would be another bus. It was after five p.m. and we realized that we might be stranded in that small village. We went into the only store in town and asked if anyone spoke English. But nobody admitted to being an English speaker and neither of us knew any Danish.

Finally, we found one woman who through pantomime figured out to call us a taxi. When the taxi arrived, the driver also spoke only Danish. We wanted to go to the train station in Odense where we had agreed to meet Ivik. Susan did her best to pantomime a train. Apparently, the choo-choo sound is not universally known. The taxi driver gave a look that was a combination of pity and disgust.

Suddenly, I remembered one Danish word. The different tracks in the train station were labeled Spor 1, Spor 2, etc. I thought *spor* must be the word for track in Danish. So I said "Odense spor." The driver seemed to understand and off we went. He drove us directly to the train station where Ivik was waiting.

We traveled by train across all of Denmark. The Danish trains were modern and smooth. They traveled at high speeds as we went from one Danish island to another over a combination of a long bridge followed by a tunnel on the ocean floor. In Odense, we met up with Ivik's sister, Pipaluk. Pipaluk was a beautiful twenty-year-old model. She had recently modeled underwear, and her sexy photos adorned the walls in one of the train stations. She was great company and made an enjoyable travel companion during our five-hour journey to Aarborg.

In Aarborg we met Ivik's grandparents, a pair of wonderful Danes who were fairly fluent in English. Because Ivik's grandparents were elderly, I insisted that we stay in a hotel in Aarborg. We shared several fine meals of Danish smorgasbord with the family. On the morning of our departure, Ivik's grandfather walked down to the hotel and paid our entire bill. It was a very bold act of kindness. After Aarborg, we returned to Copenhagen for the flight back home.

# CHAPTER TWELVE: OUR FIRST RUSSIAN ADOPTION

By this point, Susan and I had traveled across several continents, had made friends all over the world, hosted not one but two foreign exchange students, and engaged in other new activities to keep expanding the bounds of our comfort zone. But in 1997, we took an even greater leap and decided to adopt two children from a Russian orphanage. Susan always had a big heart for children, and she was particularly drawn to orphans. For more than a decade, she had wanted to adopt, but I was reluctant. Finally, when we moved to Boise, I felt like we were in the right place in terms of our health, energy, time, and finances. Both of our biological daughters were out of the house and living happy, independent lives. So together, Susan and I made the difficult decision to adopt two children. Our ages of forty-eight and forty-nine dictated that our best opportunity would be to adopt internationally.

Susan possessed a powerful love for all children and she was open to adopting any child. Selfishly, I wanted to commit to only healthy children with few problems. We began the adoption process soon after finding Roman Sergeivich Mandra's picture on the New Hope Adoption Agency website in January 1998. By March, we had found a second infant we hoped to adopt, named Angelina Borisovna Kushnaryova. Angelina was half-Uzbek, so she had Asian features, while Roman appeared fully Russian. Both were very cute infants, and Susan and I were instantly in love with our children-to-be. I was surprised by how quickly we experienced such strong emotions.

While we were waiting for our paperwork to be processed, we were told that KTVB television in Boise was planning to do a special program on Russian adoptions and wanted to interview us. We nervously agreed to the interview, although I secretly feared we would look foolish on television to all our friends and family.

The television crew arrived and filmed about one hour with us in our home. The reporter, Roland Beres, interviewed us for about thirty minutes and then conducted a tour of our home and our nursery for the new babies. We discussed our emotions and shared pictures of our children-to-be.

He asked us why we wanted to adopt children from Russia. At that time the Russian economy was so distressed that there were more than two million orphans needing homes. During the next several years, we would be asked that question again and again by family and friends. Whenever we were asked, we quietly thought to ourselves, "Why would we *not* adopt these children who need parents? Why would we *not* want to provide a loving home for innocent orphans? Why can't others see the blessings that will come to both the children and to us? If they ask this question, can they really understand the answer?" Despite our feelings, Susan and I always answered, "We want to adopt because there is a need and we want to fulfill that need."

All the filming the crew did was condensed to about eight minutes of airtime. We were one of two adopting couples that were shown in the four-part special program. Part of the taping was done in Novosibirsk, Russia. The special was titled "From Russia with Love" and was picked up by Northwest Cable News and shown two or three times on stations in Portland, Seattle, and Spokane, as well as in Boise. Since that time, several people living in Seattle, as well as several in Boise, have told us that they made an adoption decision as a result of viewing that program. Hearing about those decisions made my heart smile.

Both the New Hope representatives and the Immigration and Naturalization Service told us that we would be traveling to Russia in May to finally meet Roman and Angelina. But our paperwork was repeatedly delayed by various US agencies. Later we were told that we would certainly travel in June or July. But subsequent problems pushed back our departure even further. Now we wouldn't leave until August or September.

Meanwhile, we had learned enough about the institutionalization of infants and children to know that every second that a child remained in an

Eastern European orphanage was detrimental to that child's brain chemistry and future behavior. Both the United States and Russian bureaucrats who processed the adoption paperwork didn't seem to care about this fact. Susan and I were very frustrated by all the delays. We learned that the FBI had lost our fingerprints and had told nobody for months, hoping that they would find them and avoid the embarrassment. We drove to Montana to be fingerprinted again because the Boise office of the Immigration and Naturalization Service (INS) could not receive payments for fingerprinting. Senator Larry Craig's office helped us expedite the paperwork, and he drafted a letter for us to give to the US embassy in Moscow to ease the adoption process there.

Finally, after eleven months of paperwork, frustration, and daily telephone calls, we were able to travel—only now it was December and the Siberian winter was wrapping its icy fingers around all of Mother Russia.

Then, just two weeks before our December departure, we learned that a Russian family had adopted Angelina Kusharyova. It is difficult to describe all the disparate emotions that this news produced in us. Susan experienced a great sense of loss and she cried for many days, but at the same time we were both cheered by the knowledge that Angelina would not remain in an orphanage. So we moved forward with the adoption of Roman.

With the start of winter came bad news. Early in December, we learned that all of the four-hour flights from Anchorage, Alaska, to Magadan, Russia, were cancelled for the remainder of the year. Our travel route now snaked from Boise to Seattle to Moscow to Magadan, and then back the way we came, a total round-trip distance of 22,250 miles! This gargantuan trip would take forty-four hours.

Nevertheless, we left Boise on December 11, 1998, with our hearts full of love and our heads fearful of the unknowns that awaited us. Our first stop was Seattle, Washington, where we had to purchase tickets on Domodedovo Airlines from Moscow to Magadan. We soon learned that the Russian mafia controlled all domestic airline ticket sales within Russia. Seattle was the only US location of the one Russian mafia agency that was allowed to sell domestic Russian airline tickets at that time.

The real-life movie in which we would participate was beginning. We had never knowingly encountered professional criminals before this journey. Now we would have to work with them. Once in Seattle we followed a map to an old and seemingly abandoned building in an industrial/port area of the city. We could not believe that they sold airline tickets at this place. Once inside the old warehouse, we were directed by a small sign to a very creepy office in a back corner of an upper floor. Inside the office was a towering Russian man with dark eyes and a cold stare. He provided the tickets for cash. His conversation consisted of a few grunts. He maintained the cold stare as I left the office. Back in the safety of my car, I took a deep breath.

With our tickets in hand, we met our travel companions the next day in the Seattle airport. These people were also adopting Russian children through the same agency. They were Barbara (a single mother from Nebraska who was to adopt her second child), James (a single businessman from Atlanta, Georgia), and Joel and Susan (a couple from Washington). All turned out to be great companions and likeable people.

Our first Aeroflot experience was stressful. We knew Russian airplanes differed from American airplanes in at least two important ways: very little maintenance was performed and there were no flaps on the wings of Russian airplanes. Due to the absence of flaps, Russian airplanes were forced to take off and land at much higher speeds. But because of the lack of aircraft maintenance, Russian pilots were some of the best in the world.

Many Russian pilots also consumed alcohol heavily. On September 18, 1997, an Aeroflot aircraft with likely inebriated pilots made three attempts to land in Seattle. The pilot apparently had a problem locking onto the airport's landing signal. Also, air traffic controllers couldn't understand what the pilot was saying. The plane missed two approaches to land about a mile west of the end of Sea-Tac's runway. At one point, the noisy Ilyushin-62 came within 800 feet of the ground as it circled, alarming nearby residents. After that incident, for a time, Russian aircraft were not allowed to land at Sea-Tac airport. Needless to say, the combination of no flaps, poor maintenance, and drunk pilots made us concerned for our safety.

Almost all of the Russian passengers smoked. As soon as the no smoking sign was turned off, the entire plane became a big smoke bomb. The no smoking section had the same smoke density as the smoking section. There were constant lines to the restroom because all the Russians in the no smoking section had to go to the restroom to smoke. After waiting in line for about twenty minutes, we encountered a big sign in the restroom in both Russian and in English that said, "No standing on the toilet seat to pee."

When we arrived in Moscow, it was very early in the morning and we were exhausted from a night of little sleep in the flying smoke bomb. When we became a little more alert, we realized we had a problem. All the customs forms were in Russian and none of the customs officials at that early hour admitted to knowing any English. Nobody in our group could read Russian, so we began asking the other passengers if anyone could translate for us. We finally found a man who could help.

It was very difficult to know whether to declare our $20,000 in US cash for the adoption and risk a robbery by the police, the friends of the police, or friends of the customs officials. Our other option was to hide the undeclared cash and risk a prison term in Russia for failure to declare. Our adoption agency had advised us to declare the money, so Susan and I did so with some trepidation. We spent the next two weeks wondering if we would get robbed.

As we left the customs area in Moscow, everything changed and we walked from a deserted area into a crowded gauntlet of Russian people reaching out to us and yelling. Some were trying to get us to ride in their taxis, some wanted us to go to their hotels, and some just wanted money for guide services. Our gallant guide Sergei was also there with a large van. Sergei was the son of Zena, our New Hope adoption facilitator in Magadan, Russia. Sergei and his driver escorted us through the vociferous throngs.

Sergei was a young Russian entrepreneur who spoke English and had lived in the United States. He was an accountant by training and he had his own consulting firm in Moscow. Russia in the 1990s was a dangerous, sometimes lawless place where corruption, thuggery, and organized crime was widespread, and during his work as an accountant, he learned about 60 million tax dollars that had been skimmed off by the mafia. When he reported his finding to his employer, the mafia retaliated by having him arrested and imprisoned. He was finally released after being shown various devices of torture that would be used the next time he reported any future illegal activities.

Our Moscow hotel, the Hotel Molodyozhny, was comfortable and fairly secure, with four guards at the door and police wielding AK-47s in the lobby. All of us had to forfeit our passports when we checked into each hotel. We all hoped the passports would be returned on our departure, but there was no certainty that they would be.

The Molodyozhny was a mid-priced Moscow hotel. In typical European fashion, there were lady floor attendants to care for our keys and to act as makeshift concierges. During our three-day stay, the hotel restaurant was never open, but there were some limited food options at the bistro. We used all of our knowledge of conversational Russian to obtain a little food. My Russian was the best, so I usually spoke for the group and resolved problems between the hotel and the other guests who had abused their telephone time. There were only a few minutes in which a long distance call was free. After that minimum free period, the long distance charges were high by American standards and astronomical by Russian standards. The floor attendants were paranoid that we would run up gigantic telephone bills and then leave the hotel without paying (they were forgetting that the front desk had our passports).

While we were in Moscow, we learned that the mafia controlled every business from the smallest street vendor to the large GUM department stores. Every single business had to pay a percentage to the mafia to remain in business. People grimly accepted the situation as part of life. For many reasons, I never felt safe at any point during my time in Russia. Potential sources of danger abounded, including the police and the Russian mafia, and you sometimes weren't sure whom you could trust.

On the day we left Moscow, we faced a new crisis. We learned as we arrived at the airport for internal Russian flights that Joel and Susan did not have tickets (like the ones we bought from the Russian mafia in Seattle) but only had reservations on Domodedovo Airlines. At that time, a reservation meant nothing in Russia. Normally it took a full day to purchase a ticket due to the complex system in use there. Our court dates in Magadan were set for the following day, and if we could not all board the flight, we would all lose at least a week. None of us really wanted to spend Christmas in Siberia.

First, Sergei tried to buy tickets from the mafia at the airport on the black market. I was struck by how large these two Russian mafia men were. Broad-shouldered, and muscular these two men stood over six and a half feet tall. They stared with the same cold intensity of the man with dark eyes in Seattle.

The price of tickets was increased to $1,600 instead of the $600 normal price. Joel and Susan could not afford the extra $1,000 and insisted on buying the normal tickets. The rest of us were becoming irritated with the couple's lack of preparation and unwillingness to spend an extra $1,000.

When Sergei finally made it to the front of several different lines, he was told that all of the computers in the Moscow airport were down and no tickets would be available before the plane left for Magadan. By then, all the black market tickets were gone too. We were in severe panic mode, but Sergei remained calm and found a working telephone on which he called a friend at another airport (St. Petersburg, I think). He was able to purchase the tickets and have them printed in the Moscow airport at the last minute. But now our airplane was boarding!

The next part is a blur in my memory because two big Russian women who were weighing luggage got very mad at the Americans and started throwing our bags and yelling Russian profanities. It was a mad scramble to get tickets, bags, and separated luggage tags back from the floor and then run with them to the checked baggage location. One of Joel's carry-on bags was sent into checked luggage by mistake. Sergei had to have the belt stopped and had to run to retrieve it from the belt inside the luggage sorting area. Finally, all the bags were checked and we all ran out into a dark, frozen runway to catch our ice-covered airplane, slipping as we ran. We made it inside just before they closed the doors.

Next we had to endure a very tight and uncomfortable nine-hour flight to Magadan. Joel was a large man, and he sat with his head between his knees for the entire flight. The immensity of Russia was surprising, and from the air the dense pine forests went on seemingly for forever. The country is about 3,500 miles from north to south and about 6,800 miles from east to west. When the sun is setting on the westernmost part of Russia, it is already dawning on a new day in the eastern part.

Magadan was a city of about ninety thousand people located eight time zones east of Moscow (there are eleven time zones altogether in Russia). There were no dependable roads or railroads to Magadan. The port of Magadan was only open in the summer because even the Russian icebreakers couldn't penetrate the ice for the remainder of the year.

Stalin founded Magadan in 1939 as a port city to facilitate the transportation of prisoners to the Kolyma River region to the north. Nine of the most feared of all the Russian gulags were located in the Kolyma area. For an estimated two million prisoners, Magadan was the last city they ever saw. The prisoners either died in the inhuman gulags or on the "road of bones" as they marched to the north. Today, the Russians still know Magadan as the "gateway to hell."

When we arrived in Magadan, the temperature was minus thirty degrees Fahrenheit outside and plus thirty degrees Fahrenheit inside our apartment. Ice coated the inside of the double pane windows. Our guide and facilitator, Zena, lived in the apartment upstairs, and she arranged for James and us to stay in the vacated two-bedroom apartment of a friend downstairs. Joel and Susan and Barbara were housed in two apartments in a different building. We had to buy groceries and fix our own meals most of the time. All the REI freeze-dried food and snacks we carried came in very handy. Surprisingly, the food we bought at the stores was good and in great abundance because at that time most Russians had very little money. We had expected lines in all the stores, but because of recent inflation and a lack of buying power, there were none.

James was a Chick-fil-A executive from Atlanta, Georgia, with a very thick Southern drawl. When he talked, Zena could not understand a word he said. By the same token, because Zena's English was thickly accented, James could seldom understand her. I spent a good deal of my time acting as an interpreter between the two.

Almost every apartment in Russia had a steel door with at least three deadbolt locks. Our apartment was no exception. Our ground floor windows were barred to protect from intruders. Our apartment consisted of four small rooms, a tiny bedroom with books for Susan and me, a tiny bedroom for James, a combination living room, dining room, and kitchen area, and a very small bathroom. The bathroom would not pass the health code in most countries, even those in some Third World countries. It looked as if it had not been cleaned, painted, or maintained in at least thirty years and smelled as if some terrible events had happened there. The shower consisted of a tiny tub with a short hose. An ice cold shower could be taken if we sufficiently compressed our bodies. Most Russians in Magadan smelled of strong body odors because hot water was available only one or two days per week.

Magadan had "central heat," but that term evidently had a different meaning in Siberia. That meant that the water was heated in a central facility outside of town and then pumped through pipes to radiators in the homes and businesses. The insulation had fallen off the pipes, so water that started its journey at a boiling temperature was only slightly warm by the time it traveled seven miles in sub-freezing temperatures. Because the radiators didn't work, the citizens of Magadan often relied on inefficient electric space heaters in living areas. The electric heaters were a large drain on the precious electrical energy supplies for the city in winter. At night, we saw light coming through the cracks and holes in many of the poorly insulated apartment buildings. During winters, some people in Magadan froze to death because their homes were so frigid.

The coal supplies for the city's electrical generator were inadequate, so the electricity had to be conserved. In our neighborhood, the power was off for a total of six hours every day from 10:00 a.m. to noon, from 4:00 to 6:00 p.m., and from 10:00 p.m. to midnight. In December, the days were short, with dawn at 10:00 a.m. and sunset at 3:00 p.m. Each day at 4:00 p.m., it was completely black and all the room heaters stopped working. We had two flashlights and one candle to use during the late afternoon blackout. We were usually snuggly wrapped in bed when the 10:00 p.m. power outage turned off our heaters.

The people we met in Magadan were as warm as the country was cold. Their attitudes seemed unaffected by the minus-thirty-degree weather. Most Russians were serious people with a hard exterior shell. But when we scratched through the shell and got to know them, they were warm and loving people. Once they become your friend, they remain loyal friends for life. We met many Russian people who treated us wonderfully.

Zena was particularly great. She made life much more pleasant for us all with her cheery attitude. She had to convince all types of government officials to process our paperwork quickly. Each day we dealt with official decrees, court records, children's birth certificates, passports, and translations of everything. Each day began with a workable plan that was later met with a crisis and a corresponding scramble to get the needed documents to the right place instantly. But each day ended well because Zena was a wizard, a master at inventing a solution to each problem. In Russia it is officially illegal to give bribes, but there is no problem in giving "gifts." We gave many gifts in the form of chocolates, perfumes, and flowers.

Zena told us about a saying in the Russian language that is roughly translated as "a man must know how to give a bribe, when to give a bribe, and to whom to give a bribe or . . . he is a shit." If you made any mistake in bribing a government official, you might end up in prison for a minimum of three years before having a hearing. Bribing the military, the police, or the mafia carried the additional risk of death. Zena told us that each day was a gift and each day might be her last.

At dinnertime on three different days, we went out to a restaurant to celebrate our success. The best restaurant in town was the Green Crocodile, which sported a live croc living in the entryway. That croc must have certainly felt out of his element in this frozen land. There were about fifteen different restaurants in Magadan and all had good food and drink. We learned that

Russians make eating and drinking together a joyous event. I particularly remember a celebration with some first-class Armenian Cognac.

In another sign of Russian dysfunction, Magadan police had not been paid a salary for three months. This was not a problem because the officers parked their patrol cars at a busy intersection and "arrested" each motorist for a fabricated offense unless a "fee" was paid on the spot. Most people paid the fee to avoid the problems of going to court. Teachers and other government workers had also not been paid for many months, but they did not have any option except to survive and hope that they would be paid someday.

In Magadan, our van driver was named Ivan. He was tall, dark, and ruggedly handsome. One day Barbara was practicing her Russian with us in the van. She kept saying "yeah teh-byah loo-bloo" over and over again. It means "I love you" in Russian. She was practicing to be able to say this clearly to her new son, who was six years old. She said it many times to us and we said it sounded great, but we said, "You need to try it out on a real Russian." So without thinking and without any explanation, she shouted out to our driver, Ivan, on his return to the van: "yeah teh-byah loo-bloo." His eyes got big and he looked startled. We were roaring with laughter and Barbara thought she was saying the words incorrectly so she said it louder: "yeah teh-byah loo-bloo." Ivan turned red and was so embarrassed. We were all laughing so hard that we were crying. Later, a red-faced Ivan showed Barbara pictures of his wife and kids and we laughed some more.

One day, Zena arranged for us to have dinner at the home of the minister of education for the Magadan Region. The minister of education was a former communist party member and part of the elite class of Magadan. He had three beautiful grown daughters and lived a pleasant lifestyle. His apartment home had two steel doors with many deadbolt locks on each.

We ate dinner at an elegant table for fourteen. There was an ornate chandelier over the table and lace curtains on all the windows. Seated next to the minister on one side was his wife and on the other side was his mistress. Having a mistress at the table didn't seem unusual to anyone in the family. We all had a wonderful conversation about the world and about the similarities and differences between Russia and the United States. Zena served as translator.

The main course was salmon and the main accompaniment was crepes. Zena said the crepes were currant crepes, but we tasted them and told her they would be called huckleberry crepes in America. After dinner, each of the minister's daughters brought us rubles to exchange for several hundred American dollars. It was against the law for any private citizen in Russia to hold dollars, but it was very common among many people because the rubles were rapidly losing their value.

Only two banks in Magadan could exchange dollars for Russian rubles. Both of these banks had bars on the windows and guards in the lobby with Kalashnikov rifles. We six Americans exchanged a total of $600 for rubles at one bank. We took all the cash the bank had in rubles! Suddenly we had all the money in the bank but no bars on our windows and no security guards with automatic weapons. We all felt like we had a bull's-eye painted on us for the remainder of our time in Russia.

Each day we were allowed to visit our children in the Child's Home, the orphanage for children three years old and younger. Despite peeling paint and plaster falling from the exterior walls, the home was solidly built and brightly painted on the inside. The place smelled clean and fresh and the staff was very nice.

This was a magical and rewarding time with our new children. The children . . . I will remember the children forever! They were so tiny, so well behaved, and so innocent. We all fell in love with them immediately. It was a wonderful time to interact and play games. We were told that the food allotment was only the equivalent of one cent per child per day. When I think about the children that were never adopted, it hurts in my soul. According to the November 1999 issue of *Life* magazine, about 80 percent of the orphans in Russia later committed suicide or entered a life of crime after they were released from orphanages. There are very few more recent studies of Russian orphans because they are a great embarrassment to the country and officials are uncooperative to researchers. Nevertheless, a 2002 study of 15,000 Russian orphans who left institutional orphanages two years earlier found: about 5,000 were unemployed; 6,000 were homeless; 3,000 had committed crime; 1,500 had committed suicide; and almost half of the girls were forced into prostitution.

Only a few days in my lifetime have been as incredible as the day I first saw my new child's face. Roman was dressed in a dark shirt and tiny overalls and his eyes sparked with hope. Both Susan and I loved playing with Roman for the first time; he was very enthusiastic, and he loved most of the nutritional snacks we brought for him. He was a wonderful, intelligent child and we were amazed at how completely we loved him already.

We were also able to participate in the daily routines at the orphanage. We got to experience feeding Roman the orphanage food with a very large spoon. The daily orphanage gruel consisted of broth with mashed potatoes and, in honor of our visit, a small amount of meat. Twice a day the children ate this gruel. We were privileged to see the daily potty training in which each child was placed on a ceramic pot after the meal. All the tiny children dutifully used the pots. No diapers were used in Russia. Instead the infants and tiny children were changed every two hours. And by night they were dressed lovingly in warm and fuzzy jumpsuits since the orphanage got very cold when the power was turned off.

The best part of the trip for me came on our final day in Magadan. We dressed our children at the orphanage in American clothes (including their first time in diapers). It was surreal how these Russian babies were already taking on the appearance of tiny Americans. Then we went outside to take pictures with the caregivers and to say goodbye to the staff. It was an emotional scene: everyone cried with tears of joy and tears of loss. Finally, the van driver honked and we loaded up the children.

In my mind, I can still clearly picture the scene. The windows on the van were frosted in many patterns of ice. The sun illuminated the van through the frosted ice with a brilliant glow. Each new parent was beaming with a joy so complete. Each of us looked at each other and then at the child the other was carrying. We all felt such overwhelming satisfaction and we knew we would all remember this moment forever.

The van was traveling on an ice-covered highway to the former military airport in Sokol, about sixty kilometers north of Magadan. Russian music was blaring on the radio and the joyous feeling was suddenly so strong in us all. We were finally going to make it. Our son was going to be ours. My eyes today still fill with tears of joy. Wow . . .

The ten-hour flight back to Moscow was much easier with our children. People with infants and toddlers were allowed to board first in Russia and the larger front seats also contained built-in bassinets. The flight was also pleasant because Roman was very well behaved. He just wanted to walk, so we held his hands and had him practice assisted walking up and down the aisle.

We were happy to be back in Moscow and back in Sergei's care. We had returned to civilization and enjoyed being tourists for a day or two with our new children. We gave Roman a bath each day in the sink of our hotel. Then we visited Red Square, the site of the Winter Olympics, and many of Russia's famous onion dome Orthodox churches. We purchased a few Russian souvenirs both for us and for our children when they got older. We ate meals both at McDonalds, whose presence in the country was still a novelty after so many decades of communism, and several fine Russian restaurants. Elderly Russian women scolded us for not bundling our children more tightly, even though the temperature in Moscow was a balmy thirty-five degrees Fahrenheit. It was a Russian tradition to tightly bundle the infants, and the babushkas frowned upon violating that tradition.

Susan holding Roman in Moscow, Russia

In addition to tourism, we had more work to accomplish in Moscow. We had to take Roman to the doctor for a physical and we had to go to the US embassy to complete our paperwork before leaving Russia. The physical went very quickly and without any problems. The doctor reviewed all the Russian medical information for us. We were thankful for any medical history information we could get. The embassy visit went well, too, and we were thankful for the help from Senator Craig. Then there were more papers, more stamps, more customs officials, and finally the long flight back home from Moscow to Seattle to Boise.

Happy and exhausted, we made it home late on Christmas Eve. Both of our daughters, Kim and Alisha, met us at the airport. It was a memorable family reunion. The girls had been very busy in our absence. They cleaned our home to white glove standards and placed a big "Welcome Home Roman" banner over the door. Everyone in the family loved Roman from the beginning, and we all shared in his first unassisted steps on Christmas morning.

# CHAPTER THIRTEEN: OUR SECOND RUSSIAN ADOPTION

In late June 1999, we were preparing for a wedding for our second daughter, Alisha. The wedding was planned for July 24 and was going to be the most important event in our lives that summer. We decided to put a hold on any plans to adopt a second child and to focus our efforts on Roman because he had some special needs. Then, through a telephone call, we learned that a new baby girl had come to the Magadan Child's Home. Our friends Joel and Sue were back in Magadan adopting a second child. They told us that the new baby girl was being called the "Cavanaugh baby." They knew we had originally wanted two children and they hoped we would return for this baby girl. They sent us a video and pictures of the girl, whose name was Angelina Borisovna Lobanova. After some serious conversation, we concluded that God's plan was for this Angelina Cavanaugh baby to become part of our family.

This time the paperwork went very quickly because most of it had been completed already. We learned it might be possible to travel in July. Of course, we wanted to go as quickly as possible, but we wondered how we would do a Russian adoption and a wedding in the same month. We also had a second, more serious problem. We had no court date set for the adoption hearing. Without a court date, the adoption could not happen. Despite these problems, Zena told us to "just come to Magadan" and "we will make the adoption happen." So we perhaps foolishly put the wedding on hold and left for Russia.

This time, the airplanes were flying to Magadan from Anchorage, so we were able to shorten the trip. The air travel time from Anchorage to Magadan was just four hours, and it seemed that in that brief time we suddenly stepped back into the old movie from our first trip.

Immediately, our world changed when we landed in Magadan, Russia. In place of a modern American airline terminal was a single Russian soldier with a fur hat and an AK-47 rifle. The soldier motioned us to go toward a distant military Quonset hut made of corrugated metal. There, we discovered a pile of suitcases and tires stacked about fifty feet high. Many had purchased tires in America because Russian tires were of such poor quality. The Russians on the airplane immediately scaled the pile to pull out their respective suitcases and tires. As the pile shrunk, we eventually found our luggage.

With our suitcases in hand, it was time to go through customs. Having the knowledge that those customs officials worked for the mafia and that Magadan was the number one smuggling location in all of Russia was disconcerting. Once again we declared our $20,000 in cash and once again we worried for two weeks about our decision.

Magadan retained an air of pre-perestroika Sovietness that was reminiscent of old newsreels of the USSR. The uniform concrete buildings were painted either communist gray or some repulsive pastel color. In 1999, the time-mottled buildings bore numerous cracks, holes, and caverns. Poor construction practices combined with poor quality cement (supplied by a company the governor owned) and a lack of maintenance in the frozen taiga terrain left almost all buildings in a state of severe disrepair. However, the Russians in Magadan were working very hard in the short summer to fix and reconstruct as much as possible in preparation for the sixtieth anniversary celebration honoring the birth of the city. Outside, there were residents everywhere cleaning up the streets and parks.

Summer was so much different for this part of Russia. The ocean and countryside surrounding Magadan were stunningly beautiful. With its mountains, pine trees, plentiful berries, bears, and a beautiful ocean, Magadan looked much like Alaska. We visited the nearby Olskaya Lagoon beach twice on this trip, and we noticed that Russians at leisure were similar to Americans at leisure. Many families enjoyed the day wading, sunbathing, picnicking, drinking beer, and generally relaxing. Although Magadan is located in Asia, the Russians had a more European view of skimpy bathing suits and going topless on the beach. I was surprised that many of the Russian women were quite attractive.

In one area of Olskaya Lagoon, people were fishing for pink salmon with gill nets. The nets were set perpendicular to the shoreline and extended about five hundred feet into the bay. Spawning pink salmon trying to follow the shoreline and then migrate up the Ola River were easily caught in the nets. Fishermen in small boats pulled out the trapped salmon and hauled them to the shore.

The salmon ranged from about three pounds to more than twenty pounds in size. Some of the salmon were cleaned on site and boiled in stew pots with vegetables over wood fires on the beach. The boiling pink salmon and vegetables smelled delicious as their scent intermingled with the smoke aroma from the wood fires. I was tempted to ask for a taste, but I didn't have enough confidence in my Russian language abilities.

The gill nets did not catch all of the salmon because the Ola River was still filled with pink salmon. It was the highest salmon density I had ever seen. It appeared that a man could easily walk across the river on the backs of the salmon. (In fact, a total of 11 million pink salmon were counted in the Olskaya Lagoon in the summer of 1999).

The most interesting restaurant experience we had in Magadan was when the four of us (the two Susans, Joel, and I) dined at a North Korean restaurant. We did not take our interpreter, so we had to communicate with my rudimentary knowledge of Russian. Our Russian/English dictionary did not contain any Korean food words, so it was difficult to determine what to order. We decided to just point at items on the menu and ask for them.

The food tasted very good, although we had no idea what we were consuming. The plates were small and we had to continue ordering to satisfy our appetites. After thirty minutes, the wait staff wanted us to prove we really had the money to pay before they would allow us to order more food. We had plenty of rubles to cover our bill because the restaurant was inexpensive.

Two times while dining in Magadan, we encountered the governor of the Magadan Oblast (region or province) dining alone. Mr. Valentin Tsvetkov was a very powerful and wealthy man in that region because he controlled the concrete company that supplied the raw materials for most buildings, as well as the sidewalks, parking lots, and many roads. Mr. Tsvetkov seemed very cordial, but Zena told us that he was not well liked and there were rumors that he had fallen out of favor with the mafia. Indeed, just three years after our visit, on October 18, 2002, Mr. Tsvetkov was assassinated in Moscow in what Russian authorities believed was a contract killing by the mafia.

One of the most interesting places we visited was an elementary school in Magadan, whose contrasts with a typical American school were fascinating. The Russian children were very polite and very well mannered. The Magadan teachers were kind but much more authoritarian than their American counterparts. There was more of an "old-school" approach to education in Russia, a holdover from Soviet times. The elementary school had an amazing gymnasium with exercise facilities that would rival those of many US colleges. But the most striking facility at this Siberian elementary school was their large greenhouse/classroom. Inside the greenhouse were numerous plants from all over the world. The elementary-aged children were allowed to do experiments with the many plants, and they had classes in which they studied all the different plant forms.

We learned that after glasnost, the successor organization to the KGB was the FSB, or Federal Security Service. The headquarters of the FSB in Magadan were located in the building that was physically attached to our apartment building. Zena was always nervous about the proximity of the FSB. The Russian mafia and the FSB were virtually the same organization in 1999.

One day, Joel and I were walking together on the sidewalk to get some groceries when we noticed a black Mercedes sedan was traveling slowly parallel to us. We were quite nervous, since both of us were carrying two hundred crisp new hundred-dollar bills. The black Mercedes stayed with us for two blocks, and then as we hit an intersection, it turned in front of us and stopped. Since the car was blocking our path, we stopped, as well. Many options ran through my head, but I chose to stand relaxed, and so did Joel. The dark-tinted windows on the Mercedes were lowered, and inside the car we saw four large

Russian men wearing suits, hats, and sunglasses. All of us just stood there staring at each other for what seemed like two minutes. Then the windows went up and the car continued on its way.

We felt great relief. These were probably members of the FSB/Russian mafia and somehow we had survived the encounter. We later learned that the FSB was heavily involved in the Russian adoption process and these men likely left us unharmed to continue the business as usual.

But new frustrations were encountered when we were driving in the Magadan area in the summer. The springtime freeze/thaw cycle had badly eroded the pavement. Many of the potholes were such large caverns that our van could virtually disappear in them. Because Russian tires were of poor quality, our lady van driver had to fix three flat tires in two days of driving. She was extremely proficient in quickly changing the flat while wearing a dress and nylon stockings. It was apparent that she had had a great deal of practice. Our friends said that they went through four tires in driving sixty kilometers north to the next town. They said when their driver ran out of spare tires, he simply ran out into the road with a couple bottles of vodka and traded the vodka for extra spare tires.

I was surprised to learn in my conversations with the Russian people that they possessed a strong fear of Americans. Growing up in the 1950s and 1960s, we were told to fear the Russians. We were told they were the aggressors. Now I learned that the Russian people feared us. They posted guards who were constantly watching the horizon, half-expecting American soldiers to come over the mountains to attack their city at any moment. This deep fear is due to more than just propaganda (although media brainwashing has played a role). It is also the consequence of a history of invasion caused by the absence of natural geographical boundaries. Russia has been repeatedly attacked and partially conquered by Mongolian, Swedish, Polish, French, Japanese, and, most notably, German invaders. This history of conflict has given rise to a survival instinct in the Russian people. They are constantly fearful for their safety, and this fear has led to an emphasis on a controlling government, communal goals, distrust of other countries, a belief in preponderant military strength, and "defensive" expansion of their boundaries. Fear can do bad things to a society.

One of the most striking places to view the city of Magadan was from the 600-foot-high Krylaya Hill, where the large sculpture "The Mask of Sorrow" is located. The famed sculptor Ernst Neizvestny designed the forty-eight-foot-high concrete statue of a face with tears coming from the left eye in the form of small masks. The right eye is in the form of a barred window. Inside the statue is a replica of a Stalin-era prison cell. On the backside of the statue, there is a headless man on a cross and a weeping woman. The statue was unveiled only three years before our arrival in Magadan. The purpose of the statue was to commemorate the many prisoners who suffered and died in the gulag prison camps of the Kolyma region of the Soviet Union during the 1930s through 1950s. At this monument, the names of the nine gulag camps are set in stone, and stone monuments to all of the world's great religions are set like grave markers.

As I looked down, the city of Magadan was illuminated by the setting sun and fringed on two sides by ocean bays sparkling like jewels. There was so much peace in this place and yet indescribable sadness, as well. The monuments were a reminder of the terrible acts that were so common during Stalin's rule. I then asked Zena how many people went to the gulags through Magadan. She just stared at her feet and with great difficulty said, "Many . . . many . . ."

Zena told us of a time when her excellent English skills had earned her a position as a tour guide for Alaska Airlines. A trip was organized by the airline to the Kolyma region to see one of the gulags. Zena was the guide and interpreter for the only group of tourists to view the camp. They traveled to Bulygychag, where political prisoners were mining uranium ore and were exposed to high levels of radiation.

The Alaska Airlines jet landed in the small runway and everybody disembarked. A heavy sense of death and despair permeated the air. The black sky reflected the black ground. The terrible feelings of that grim place have never left her, she said. After that single trip, Alaska Airlines made a decision not to take any more tourists to any of the Kolyma labor camps.

While we were in Magadan, we were able to watch the sixtieth anniversary celebration of the city's founding by Stalin in 1939. Many honored guests from Moscow, including governmental and military dignitaries, were invited to attend. The celebration lasted just two days on the weekend. The main event on Saturday was a large parade with thousands of participants. The only people in the parade that we knew were the doctors and nurses from the orphanage.

Several observations struck me as I watched the parade. First, it was apparent that despite all their struggles and hardships, the Russian people had a great deal of pride in their country. Military dignitaries were treated with great honor and respect. Russians really love their medals, and some military officers must have difficulty moving under the weight of all their decorations. Secondly, there are so many different military, police, and quasi-military groups in Russia that it seemed that every other male was in some sort of military or police service.

On Sunday, there was an outdoor presentation in the stadium to celebrate the entire history of the city. It began with Inuit groups portraying the way the region was before the white Russians arrived. Russian Inuit people seemed much like those of the United States and Canada in both appearance and costumes. Animal skin clothing, dancing, and a stimulating trampoline-like blanket toss were exhibited. Later, groups portrayed the Stalin era in which the prisoners came through the city. All Russians seemed to recognize the fact that the Stalin era was a regrettable time. The next group portrayed Russian transformation though *glasnost* (openness) and *perestroika* (restructuring). Later, the performances showed the mafia controlling the government and the country. Finally, the modern era in which the government regained control and a new and free and happy Magadan was portrayed. Most people told us privately that the portrayal was not true and that the mafia was still in control of the government and the country.

The director of the Child's Home in Magadan was named Galena. She ran the orphanage with the love and care of a grandmother and concerned physician. Everything was kept clean and spotless. There were only seventy-two children in the orphanage and many caregivers, doctors, nurses, and social workers. Because of her leadership, the Magadan Child's Home was one of the finest in Russia.

During our stay, Galena had us over for cake and tea. We all sat at a big table with a nice lace tablecloth and the requisite chandelier. The tea was very formal and Galena did a great job of making us all comfortable as we discussed the needs of the orphanage and the direction she saw the orphanage going. After our adoption, Susan and I financially assisted various orphanages in Russia, including the Child's Home in Magadan.

Angelina was truly a little angel when we first saw her in the Child's Home. She was such a calm and peaceful baby with an unmistakable aura of love surrounding her. She almost instantly bonded with both of us, and we enjoyed holding her closely and giving her kisses. She was very healthy and happy and never seemed to cry. Both Susan and I were immediately in love with our Angelina and we wanted to spend as much time as possible with her.

When we arrived in Magadan, we learned that not having a court date was a larger problem than we had been told. Criminal trials in the Magadan region were not being conducted promptly enough in 1999. Innocent people languished in prison for up to three years before they even had a hearing. Three years was a long time in a cold Siberian prison. So in typical convoluted Russian fashion, the government leaders took swift action and fired all the judges for the Magadan region except one. Of course, this only served to further jam up the court system. Hence, the process of obtaining a court date for an adoption was going to be more than a little difficult.

The day before our meeting with the judge, we went to the Russian Orthodox church to pray for help. There were a number of people begging on the steps of the church, and we gave each of them some money. Russians believe that giving money to the poor brings good fortune. We said our prayers and lit candles in the church. Even with God on our side, we were very concerned about the coming day. (But we learned in the end that God was on our side.)

It was difficult to even book an appointment to see the lone remaining judge. Zena managed to schedule a meeting, but the judge's clerk told her that the meeting would serve no purpose. For about thirty minutes, the lady judge told us via Zena's interpretation why it would be impossible to have a court date soon and that we could return in some months when the court schedule might be less busy. We were all devastated, and both Susans started crying and begging the judge to reconsider. The judge had been stern and officious, but at the sight of all the crying, she, too, became very upset. Russians are conditioned to be stoic. Outbursts of emotion are frowned upon; during the Stalin era, they could even bring about grave consequences. Russians especially never show their emotions in public. So having two crying women in her chambers was more than this judge could handle. Her Honor finally relented and agreed to allow a court date on Friday. We were all so very happy at this news! It was an answer to all our prayers.

But the next morning when we met the usually upbeat Zena, we found her in tears. She said that there was no possible way that we could get all of the documents we needed, including the children's new birth certificates and passports, on Friday afternoon after our court date. All the Russian government offices were closed on Saturday and Sunday. To stay on schedule, we absolutely had to catch an airplane to Moscow on Monday at the latest because the only day of the week for processing adoptions at the US embassy was Tuesday (thank you, US government). The more we discussed our situation, the more we realized how hopeless it was to keep our schedule. So Susan and I reluctantly made tentative arrangements to give a Russian and US power of attorney to Joel and Susan and to return home to Boise for our daughter's wedding. We would have our friends take Angelina to Seattle where we would meet, hopefully within about one or two weeks.

Zena said it might be possible to get the new birth certificates on Friday and the other necessary papers and translations, as well—if we could bribe the right people. But it was impossible to get the passports. The new chief of police for Magadan was the only person who could issue passports, and he was known to be a very dangerous and difficult man. Many people had already been sent to prison for trying to influence this chief. We trembled at the thought of spending three years in a grim Siberian prison.

I asked Zena, "Isn't there anything that is so valuable that the police absolutely need in Magadan?" Zena said, "No there is nothing." But then Zena had an idea. She told us that the most valuable item in Magadan was airline tickets. At that time, airplane tickets could not be purchased at the airport or anywhere else in the Magadan region except from the governor's office. Valentin Tsvetkov, the governor of Magadan, controlled all the sales of airline tickets. And there was no way to get in and out of Magadan except by air. In the winter, no ships could penetrate the thick ice and no trucks could transit the impassible roads. The governor's monopoly helped further consolidate his power.

Fortunately, one of Zena's friends was a secretary to the governor, and she owed Zena a favor, so perhaps airplane tickets could be obtained and maybe an arrangement might be made with the chief of police to exchange tickets for two passports. It was a very risky idea. Our brave Zena called and made arrangements to meet with the chief of police at his home late that evening. She obtained two airline tickets from her secretary friend. But she would not give us any details of that evening meeting. The next morning, she let us know that the chief of police had agreed, or at least she hoped he had agreed.

Our time in court went smoothly on Friday and we were able to complete all the other necessary paperwork by late Friday evening. The children's passports were to be obtained on Saturday when the office of the chief of police was officially closed. On Saturday morning, our hearts were beating rapidly when we arrived at the office of the chief of police. We did not know what would happen. In an instant, we could easily be arrested and put in prison.

Finally, we were allowed in the office. The door was immediately locked behind us. We were white with fear as we stepped forward to the reception desk. A secretary appeared and asked why we were there, as if she did not already know. Zena spoke very quickly in Russian and the secretary said, "One moment." The secretary pretended not to know anything about what was happening, but she leaned forward and said in a very quiet whisper, "Give me your papers." Zena again spoke quickly about the weather and she placed the papers on the counter. The secretary walked by and then deftly snatched up the papers.

The secretary went into the next office. We waited and watched silently, our hearts pounding so loudly we thought they might echo down the hallway. After about thirty minutes, the same secretary went to another office. After an hour, the secretary went to the last office on the corridor: the office of the chief of police. Then the secretary worked her way back from office to office over a two-hour time period. There was no sound. We finally figured out that the procedure was to fool any cameras or listening devices that were in the police station for surveillance. Eventually, the secretary said only in Russian, "Here are your papers back." Included at the bottom of the stack of our original papers were the new children's passports! The front door was unlocked and we exited the building. We finally could breathe! Zena had done it: the impossible!

With our passports and two children in hand, we left and made it to the airport with thirty minutes to spare to catch the airplane for Moscow. The flight to Moscow was again very comfortable and Angelina was a perfect angel. When we arrived in Moscow, there was a big surprise for us. Moscow had stifling heat and humidity. I had never thought of Moscow as hot before, but it felt just like Miami because of the humidity. I think the temperature in degrees Fahrenheit was in the nineties.

We stayed in the Hotel Rossiya across the street from the Kremlin, the second largest hotel in the world, with 3,200 rooms, 245 half-suites, a post office, a health club, a nightclub, and a movie theater. It was easy to get lost inside because the hallways twisted and turned in a maze-like fashion. The massive structure was demolished in 2007 and no building yet has taken its place.

We were happy to again be in Moscow. We went out with Angelina and found an English-speaking guide who gave us a great tour of the Kremlin and all of Red Square. He told us that most people in Moscow were working two or three jobs to make ends meet. Moscow is much different from rural Russia. It is a very pleasant city with European architecture, parks, trees, and the beautiful Moscow River. We got some reminders of current events when we went to the US embassy, where workers were trying to remove the paint and debris from the outside walls thrown by protesters opposed to US bombing in the former Yugoslavia. Happily, the physical examination and embassy work went very smoothly for us and for Joel and Susan.

While we were in the Moscow airport awaiting our departure, we had another interesting experience. From out of nowhere, a tall and handsome man approached us and began a conversation. His English was perfect, but he had a British accent, almost like James Bond. This man with perfect English joked with us and then little by little asked why we were in Moscow. We told him we were there to adopt our children and do the paperwork at the US embassy. He said that what we were doing was "very noble." He then told us several more jokes before noting that our entire luggage was sealed by the Russian security in thin red tape. He laughed and said, "That must be where they get the expression—tied up in red tape." Then he walked away. We were certain afterward that he was an agent for the FSB/mafia and was checking to see what we were doing. Since the Russian mafia was making money on adoptions, the practice was allowed. This last encounter was the ending to the movie. We had passed the final test.

We then had a nice long flight home. We flew directly over Greenland and enjoyed seeing from up above the beautiful homeland of our exchange student, Ivik. Throughout all our adventures, Angelina was a little angel. She was well named and we loved her as much as all our other children. It seemed as if she had always been our child. We arrived home just three days before Alisha's wedding. The wedding was made all the better by having our wonderful new daughter with us.

Kim helping Angelina (Tia) to stand

All of us have a comfort zone. It is the area in our minds in which we feel safe and protected—that mental space where our activities and behaviors fit a routine and pattern that minimize stress and risk. Many of us are very happy to stay warm and cozy in that mental box. There, we don't have to confront our fears or do anything that is unfamiliar or difficult. It is a safe and happy place. Staying in our comfort zone comes with a price, however. The longer we stay, the smaller our comfort zone becomes. It is as if there were outside pressure pushing against the walls and shrinking this place of mental tranquility. Further, when we stay in our comfort zone, we also find that remaining stagnant is unfulfilling. We might notice that we are sometimes bored, self-critical, anxious, and envious of others.

Part of our growth as humans requires "experiential stretching," which we gain by leaving our comfort zone. When we push ourselves into the discomfort zone, we give ourselves a dose of anxiety and stress. Anxiety and stress, when taken in small doses, help us to grow. The more often we leave our comfort zone, the more comfortable we become outside of that zone. Our body and our mind make the necessary adjustments and our comfort zone gets larger. By leaving our comfort zone and then returning to that place to process, we eventually become more productive and more creative. We are better equipped to handle the unexpected changes in the future.

Our adoptions ended a decade of really stepping out of our comfort zone in a big way. We did many things in the 1990s that we wouldn't have considered doing ten years before. Our comfort zone expanded as a result of all our new experiences. Now Susan and I thought we would be ready for anything. The next decade would really put that notion to the test.

# The 2000s:
## Embracing Death is a Part of Life

"There is something about death that is comforting. The thought that you could die tomorrow frees you to live your life now."

—*Angelina Jolie*

# CHAPTER FOURTEEN: OUR WAR WITH CANCER

*Time* magazine called the 2000s (the first decade of the second millennium AD) the "decade from hell." It was a time filled with wars, acts of terrorism, recessions, stock market crashes, financial scandals, antitrust cases, and other disasters. In some ways, it was the worst decade for both the United States and the world since the end of World War II.

The decade began with twenty different African factions engaged in the Second Congo War or "Africa's World War." A total of 3.8 million people died in the Second Congo War and many more millions of people were displaced from their homes. Then, on September 11, 2001—a date etched in the memories of most Americans—hijackers turned commercial airlines into missiles that leveled the World Trade Center towers and destroyed part of the Pentagon. A total of 2,996 people were killed in the first major attack on American soil since WWII. In retaliation for the attacks, a US-led coalition overthrew the Taliban government of Afghanistan, which harbored al-Qaeda, the terrorist network that had staged the assaults. On March 20, 2003, the United States and a coalition of Allies went to war against Iraq. In 2004 an earthquake in the Indian Ocean triggered a tsunami that killed more than 230,000 people and displaced more than one million from their homes.

The dotcom bubble burst in 2000 and by 2003, about 60 percent of the stock value in the NASDAQ index had been lost. In 2008, the collapse of the US housing market triggered a global financial crisis that forced governments to intervene to save major financial institutions. The United States and the world economy is still trying to recover from that financial and economic disaster.

There was also some good news in the 2000s. Facebook helped usher in a new, innovative era of social media. For minorities in the United States, it was also a decade of firsts: the first woman winner of an Indy race, the first Hispanic member of the Supreme Court, the first female speaker of the house, and the first African-American president.

For our family, the decade of the 2000s was in many ways also the "decade from hell." We were now living in Boise, Idaho, in our fifties, and raising two young children. Susan was an expert homemaker and mother, but in this decade she didn't have the energy she had when Kim and Alisha were tiny. I was never skilled at domestic duties, and I didn't have much practice because Susan handled the bulk of those the first time around. I, too, was in my fifties, so I got tired more easily. Roman and Tia were so active and demanding as babies and toddlers that both Susan and I were exhausted at the end of each day.

We realized almost immediately that both children were extremely difficult to parent and that they both exhibited behaviors that were not normal for children of their age. Tia had a brother who tormented her when we were not watching. Gradually, Tia had to become strong and athletic because she was truly afraid of Roman. Roman showed many signs of attachment disorder. He resisted comforting and nurturance. We noticed he avoided eye contact with everyone, even with his own reflection in the mirror. He easily became enraged over the smallest provocation. He looked sad almost all the time. He did not reciprocate our holding and he turned his head away when face-to-face. He did not return smiles and had little imitative behavior. He also showed a high tolerance for pain.

We obtained books on the subject of attachment and tried "holding therapy" with him, which seemed to help but did not resolve all the problems. Both Susan and I also attended classes on attachment disorder and reactive attachment disorder. The classes helped us understand Roman's behaviors and they helped us devise strategies to help him. But the problems persisted.

As Roman grew older, he was sometimes oppositional and defiant. He had outbursts of anger and was sometimes destructive to his sister, our pets, and our property. He hoarded food and seemed to have very poor relationships with other children. On top of that, he became preoccupied with fire and was very bossy with his peers.

For five years, our pediatrician was an old-school disciplinarian. He believed that both Roman and Tia were "normal," but they misbehaved because Susan and I did not discipline sufficiently. The doctor did not listen when we told him that we disciplined the two children daily. We also rewarded their good behavior in every way we could conceive. Yet no rewards or punishments seemed to modify their bad behaviors.

Our frustration was quite high when we took Roman in to see a different child behavior specialist, Dr. L., for a diagnosis. Dr. L. diagnosed Roman as having both attachment disorder and Asperger's syndrome. We were so relieved to finally have a diagnosis that made sense. This was just the first step in solving Roman's problems. We still had to deal with daily defiant behaviors and rages and still had to try various psychiatric drugs to keep him calm so we could regain our energy and sanity.

The main reason we were able to maintain our positive attitude and do our best with the children during this period was the wonderful help we received from our family and friends who lived in Boise. The saying that "it takes a village to raise children" proved very true for us. Alisha and Rob were particularly helpful, and they would support us in many ways whenever we had a need. We developed a few friends who had also adopted children and we learned from them many techniques to help raise our children more lovingly.

In January of 2002, Susan and I suddenly decided to move to Sequim, Washington. Our family and friends were shocked by our quick decision. In retrospect, it was not one of our wisest ideas. We had only two motivations to move to Sequim: to be closer to Kim and Steve (who had completed graduate school and were now living and working in Federal Way, Washington) and to eliminate our Idaho state income taxes (because Washington has no state income taxes). By moving, we failed to achieve either of these goals. Sequim is located about two hours from Federal Way, so we didn't see Kim and Steve any more often than we did when we lived in Boise. And during our four years in Washington, we incurred many unplanned expenses that exceeded our income tax savings.

At the time, Roman was five years old and Tia was barely four. Our move turned out to be a mistake because we didn't have the same support system in Washington, and we were relocating our very young and challenging children into a new environment. Consequently, both Susan and I experienced considerable stress. Because we had to be present with the children 24/7 and because we were older, we both found that we didn't always have the energy to hold everything together and to continue to be good parents. Finding childcare in a new town also was difficult because our special needs children were so difficult to babysit. Our babysitters would seldom return for a second and third time, even if we were paying more than other parents. So we had to settle for less-qualified childcare workers. The best babysitters had plenty of work and didn't need to work for us.

While facing the challenges of parenting, Susan and I learned to enjoy living in Sequim. The people of Sequim were very kind and it was easy to make friends. Gradually we made friends with parents of our children's playmates and we made some special friends in Port Angeles through our landscaper. We were so thankful to have all these friends in Sequim because they became our support network. The kids started attending schools and Tia did particularly well at the Five-Acres Elementary school, a Montessori school in the country whose curriculum included horseback riding. The kids loved going to the beach and finding shells and sea creatures. Tia loved catching frogs, snakes, and birds near our home. In Washington, the climate was wonderful for most of the year and the abundantly beautiful plant life filled the air with life-giving oxygen. We initiated a massive landscaping project that involved the construction of seven waterfalls outside our home and the planting of hundreds of trees and flowers everywhere. After two years, our verdant home was fit for inclusion in *Better Homes and Gardens*. We also purchased a twenty-six-foot Glacier Bay boat and enjoyed our time out on the water. Gradually, we were becoming acclimated to this new "village."

Boat cruise with dear friends on Puget Sound. Left to Right: Susan Cavanaugh, Carol Simon-ich, Gary Simonich, and Patrick Cavanaugh

In 2003, we purchased a condominium at the Wailea Beach Villas in Maui, Hawaii. It was scheduled to be completed in 2005 and was located just a few hundred feet from Wailea Beach. We loved the condo, and Susan and our sister-in-law, Rochelle, enjoyed decorating and furnishing the new home. We travelled to Maui about twenty times during the next five years in which we owned the property, and all our family and many friends enjoyed wonderful vacations at the condo.

Despite our gradual acclimation to Sequim, we missed our family and friends in Boise and decided that a move back to Boise would be best for every-one. Grand miracles were happening in the Idaho capital. In 2002, Alisha gave birth to our first grandchild, Shydyn. Three years later our second grandchild, Kya, was born, and in 2008, our third grandchild, Huxly, was born.

Finally, in August of 2006, we moved back to our old house in Boise. We were elated to be once again so close to our family, friends, and especially our grandchildren. We had returned to the village that had been so supportive and nurturing to our family. We had returned *home*.

It took some time to recover from our move. We were just getting back to normal during Christmas break when we took another trip to Hawaii. While we were on Maui, Susan was performing her normal five-mile circuit run/walk workout each day. She noticed that she could not run up the stairs from our condo to the upper pool area as easily as she had done in the past. She also noticed that there was one tiny blurred spot or floater in the upper corner of one eye when she looked forward. So she decided to get her eye checked out when we returned to Boise in January.

Beautiful Cavanaugh women: Susan, Kim, and Alisha

The first indication that Susan might have a serious health issue emerged when she went to her eye doctor during the second week of January 2007. The doctor was not sure why she saw a blurred spot, but he saw some cloudiness in her vitreous, the clear jellylike substance that filled the center of her eye, so he recommended that she have an ultrasound to check her eye further.

The test results were a shock: they indicated that Susan had a tumor that was likely cancerous. The eye doctor was unbelievably callous when he gave us the news, saying, "Well, none of us gets out of this life alive!" The eye doctor recommended that we go to Susan's family physician for follow-up testing.

During the next seven to ten days, Susan underwent a series of scans and tests. Her oncologist at the St. Luke's Mountain States Tumor Institute (MSTI) was a young doctor. She gave us the results of all the tests in a blunt, matter-of-fact manner: they were all terrible! Susan had stage IV breast cancer throughout her body. In addition to the tumor in Sue's eye, the cancer was everywhere. Hundreds of tumors were discovered in Sue's lungs. Tens of tumors were observed in Sue's liver. Many more tumors were found in Sue's bones. There was a large tumor in Sue's breast. Fourteen tumors existed in her brain. The prognosis was also terrible. The oncologist gave her six months to live—but added that Sue might only last a few weeks if her cancer type was aggressive. The two experienced MSTI nurses in the room were crying buckets of tears. Susan and I were crying too.

It felt like we were hit in the face with a baseball bat, repeatedly. Every time we would think about it, here came that bat in the face again. My feelings of despair were overwhelming. I called my friend Dan and the pastor of my church on my cell phone, tears flowing as I told them the news. I cried again when Susan and I told Kim and Alisha. We decided to just tell Roman and Tia that Sue was very sick. I tried to be optimistic and supportive in those first few days, but I failed miserably—especially when we learned that Sue's cancer type *was* highly aggressive.

Susan was devastated by the diagnosis for three days. Then, everything about Susan changed completely. She woke up on the morning of the fourth day after the diagnosis with a big smile on her face. That smile would be on her face every day—for the rest of her life. She said that Jesus had come to her in a dream. He told her that he would protect her on her journey and that everything would be all right. He told her that she would live as long as was necessary, and then he would carry her with him to another world. Jesus said to her that he would protect Roman and Tia too. Sue believed with every cell in her body that the voice in her dream was really that of Jesus. I certainly did not argue with her. Her attitude made a great difference in the way she lived her life from that moment forward.

Once our attitudes shifted, we became proactive regarding Sue's treatment. I began to research every possible treatment for breast cancer, including clinical, holistic, and diet-related treatments. Sue started on a daily regimen of drinking Diana's phytochemical supershake described in the book *A Dietitian's Cancer Story*. Because Sue's cancer was the type of breast cancer that contained the Human Epidermal Growth Factor 2 (HER 2) she was eligible for treatment with Trastuzumab (or the trade name Herceptin). Use of Trastuzumab increased the effectiveness of chemotherapy in HER2 patients by using their own immune systems to help in the cancer fight.

The last three letters in Trastuzumab indicate that it is a monoclonal antibody treatment produced in a laboratory. The process to make Trastuzumab begins by fusing a bone marrow cancer cell together with a mouse or rabbit B cell that can make a specific antibody that recognizes a specific antigen. The resultant fused cell is called a hybridoma. Millions of clones or exact copies of the hybridoma become the monoclonal antibodies in Trastuzumab. Monoclonal antibodies are, therefore, cloned copies of antibodies that bind specifically to certain cancer cells.

Sue began the chemotherapy and radiation therapy at MSTI and she began to take 1,3 beta-glucan daily to maximize the effects of the Herceptin on her tumors. Certain complex sugar molecules, such as 1,3 beta glucan, were proven to be effective as helpers or adjuvants with cancer treatments using monoclonal antibodies. The reason 1,3 beta glucan helped so much is because it mimicked a yeast infection and caused her immune system to work at a maximum rate fighting the perceived infection. With Herceptin binding to the enemy cancer cells and effectively marking them as the bad guys, Sue's amped-up immune system worked better to kill the cancer.

Susan also took 21 mg of melatonin daily to increase the effects of the chemo on her cancer cells and at the same time protect her healthy cells from harm. A large number university and hospital studies validated the use of melatonin in these two roles. By March 16 (sixty days from the diagnosis), Susan had secured as her lead oncologist the premier breast cancer doctor at MSTI.

In late March and early April 2007, Susan and I traveled to Santiago, Chile, to attend Cristian's wedding. Upon our return, I wrote in our journal, "The wedding was an awesome event held at the farm home of Cristian's family in Pirque, Chile. The day was perfect, the setting was magnificent, the food was phenomenal, and the family was wonderful. I was allowed to speak at the wedding and the entire audience cried with tears of joy."

Upon our return from Chile, Susan was scheduled for a routine MRI scan of her head. Her doctors were shocked by the results! The doctors had hoped that the chemo and radiation had slowed the growth of the fourteen tumors in Sue's brain. In the most optimistic case, they wished that the tumors would shrink. The results were amazing—all the tumors in Susan's brain and the tumor in her eye were undetectable on the MRI. They had disappeared completely! We returned home for just one week and then our whole family traveled to Maui for two weeks. All this time, Sue had an incredible attitude. She was fully at peace with whatever happened. She trusted that God was in control of her life. Her fortitude and optimism lifted all of us and gave us all strength.

In the middle of April, Sue had a new CT scan of her body. The results of the CT scan were also miraculous! All of the more than one hundred tumors in Sue's lungs had disappeared completely. Of the four tumors in Sue's liver, the two large ones had disappeared and only two tiny tumors remained. This was the best possible response to treatment that the doctors could have imagined. Although we did not have any information on the cancer in Susan's bones, the doctors said that the response there likely would have mirrored the response in the lungs and liver. The doctors, Sue, and I were all elated.

Susan retained her positive attitude throughout the treatments. She said she had little pain or nausea but was a little tired at times. Often, she reminded me that "Each day is a gift," and I agreed. Our family spent much of the summer in Maui to take full advantage of each precious day. We arranged to have Sue receive her chemo treatments at the hospital in Maui. It was a crowded chemo room, but it was functional and much preferred to returning to the mainland.

Upon our arrival back in Idaho in late July, we continued to receive encouraging news regarding Sue's tumors. New scans showed that they were still gone in her hipbone and brain! These had been the areas of greatest concern to the doctors. We spent the end of the summer in Sequim, and everyone was so surprised at how good Susan looked and acted. The August scans showed a further reduction in the tiny remaining tumors in Susan's liver. We were super busy with constant company, the kids, school, and travel activities, but we had won the first battle in the war with cancer.

In October 2007, Susan was feeling fine, and we traveled to Italy with Sue's brother David and his wife Rochelle on a whirlwind tour of Milan, Verona, Padova, Venice, Florence, Pisa, Assisi, Siena, Ravenna, Perugia, Sorrento, Pompeii, Capri, and Rome. The trip might have been more tiring for me than Susan. She was a real trouper. But then, in October, we got the first bad news since the original diagnosis. The cancer had returned to Susan's brain. Eight or nine small tumors had emerged in a part of her primitive brain.

We spent Christmas in Hawaii, where the kids and grandchildren all put on a wonderful talent show for us. Sue continued to feel very well and we all enjoyed watching the whales from our condo. By January 2008, the new scan reports were generally good. The tumors in Sue's brain had not grown and the tumors in her lungs, liver, and bones were still undetectable.

But the chemotherapy was taking a toll on Susan. In late February, Susan fell asleep while driving home with Roman. She crossed the highway and crashed into a pile of rocks. When I arrived, our crumpled Honda Odyssey minivan was standing vertically against the rock pile. Fortunately, Susan was not injured because the air bag held her securely. But Roman had broken his arm and thumb and was rushed to the hospital via ambulance. Roman endured painful surgery to repair the breaks and insert pins and screws the following week.

In early March, we learned that the tumors in Susan's brain were growing again. The chemotherapy combined with the monoclonal antibody treatments were working very nicely on the tumors in the rest of Sue's body, but the chemo could not get through the blood/brain barrier to fight the cancer in her brain. So Susan began new radiation treatments on her brain in March 2008. By April 2008, she had declined physically to a great extent. She was unable to move without crutches and she fell several times.

On April 18, we learned that the cancer from her brain had entered her spinal cord, where four ugly new tumors appeared. The news was devastating for me to hear. Our team of doctors told us that having cancer in a spinal cord is rare and almost always immediately fatal. Treatment is very difficult to perform because the smallest mistake will cause death.

In contrast, Sue was not worried. She smiled and told the doctors that curing the cancer in her spinal cord is "easy peasy" for God. The doctors performed a difficult and risky spinal tap treatment that they hoped would help. The treatments worked, and in May Susan's legs began to get stronger. The radiation treatments (combined with melatonin intake to protect against negative effects on the good cells) were effective. Susan knew she would get better. The radiation oncologist began to call Susan his "superstar."

In late May, Susan's white blood cell count returned to levels at which chemotherapy could be reinstituted. As a result of the treatments, Susan's energy returned and she was able to walk without assistance. However, the treatments began to produce side effects in Susan. She had extensive blistering on her extremities from radiation recall. Still, Susan's attitude was positive and our family returned to Maui in the summertime. In July, Susan had a fairly bad case of shingles but told everyone that she felt no pain from the disease. Her indomitable pain tolerance and her indefatigable attitude amazed all of us.

In August 2008, Susan and I traveled with her sister and her sister's husband on a Viking River Cruises trip to Belgium, Netherlands, Germany, France, and Switzerland. We had a wonderful time and Susan thoroughly enjoyed the trip. She felt great most of the time, although she was confined to a wheelchair for long walks. We both learned that the cobblestone streets of Europe are not compatible with wheelchairs. Shock absorbers should be added on that continent!

In October 2008, we were hit with more bad news. The tumors in Susan's brain were growing and she had nausea, weakness, and difficulty in balance and walking. Our oncologist put Susan on a new and experimental drug that had never before been used to treat metastatic breast cancer in the United States (although there were some promising results from a small study in Italy). The new treatments appeared to be working and Susan again felt much better, so our family again left to spend Christmas in Maui. This was our eighth trip to Hawaii in two years.

In January 2009, Susan was still limping around, but she remained as active as possible. In February, we hosted our former exchange student,

Cristian Franzani, and his brother Ignacio in Boise as our guests. It was enjoyable watching the great Spanish-speaking communicator and Chilean television personality, Ignacio Franzani, struggle to communicate in English. We all laughed and laughed.

The results of Susan's many scans in late February showed that the cancer tumors remained undetectable in her spinal cord, bones, lungs, and liver. No scans were conducted of Susan's brain because the doctors had run out of treatments for the brain.

During early spring, Susan began an anticancer diet and her mobility increased somewhat. She continued to be free from any pain. By late May, Susan was walking with a walker along the beach in Maui and she beamed a broad smile to inspire everyone she met. Total strangers told us that she was a shining example of love for everyone.

In midsummer, we returned from Hawaii and left immediately for Sequim. After our visit in Sequim, we left for Idaho Falls and then Susan had a reunion with her Ya Ya high school friends in Star Valley, Wyoming. As fall approached, I realized that the constant travel, the pressure of the children, and constant stress of Sue's illness were taking a toll on me. I was becoming moody and occasionally depressed. One of the reasons I was able to continue was due to the tremendous help, support, and family love given by our "family assistant," Ashley Yamada. Ashley was wonderful with the kids, and her gourmet meals were always delicious and nutritious. In almost every way, Ashley became part of our family.

Susan continued to have a great attitude when we celebrated her three-year survival since her January 2007 diagnosis. Sue was slowing down in her abilities to walk and in her energy, but her positive attitude never wavered. In late March and early April 2010, we traveled to Idaho Falls to celebrate my father's ninetieth birthday. Susan stayed in a separate motel room with Tia. In the room, Susan fell down and had difficulty getting up. She was dazed and disoriented, so we took her to the emergency room of the Idaho Falls Hospital. The doctors had no idea what had caused the problems.

In Boise, the doctors at MSTI determined that Susan had a hypothyroid problem and may have also been experiencing some dehydration. They thought her thyroid was not producing enough hormones as a result of the radiation or chemotherapy treatments and advised stopping her chemo treatments to let her body heal. They didn't admit that there might be another cause.

The tumors in Susan's brain were growing. By late April 2010, Susan was not improving. In fact, she was going downhill and was now confined to her wheelchair. From that point forward, Sue began a slow and steady decline in health. She began to sleep all but a few hours each day. Some days she was not present mentally. But always, always she was gentle and loving with everyone. We started having two caregivers in the house all day and all night. Roman and Tia had difficulty adjusting to all the changes and the decline in their mother. Roman stayed in his room most of the time, coming out only to give hugs to his mother or eat meals. Tia started misbehaving at every opportunity, especially in the evening when she was tired.

In July, our oncologist determined that the treatments would no longer help fight her disease. We began hospice care immediately. Susan moved to a hospital bed in the living room. Our caregivers helped her with all her needs. I was free to leave the house as needed.

On Friday, September 24, 2010, the morning began as just another ordinary day. Susan seemed to be doing okay sleeping, so I left for my office to complete some urgent paperwork. Late in the morning, I had a strange experience. I accidently pocket dialed Susan's former best friend in Billings. Carol Simonich answered the phone and said, "Pat . . . is everything all right?" I said, "Yes. I . . . guess I just accidently dialed your number." Carol hesitated for a minute and then in a trembling voice said, "You had better get home and check on Sue." Suddenly I had the strange feeling too. I knew something was different—something had happened.

As I drove home, my telephone rang and one of the caregivers said I should get home right away. When I arrived home, the hospice nurse told me that Sue had died. I rushed to her and hugged her and kissed her goodbye. Both the caregivers were deeply shaken by the experience of watching Susan die. I didn't know what to say to them. For me, everything was spinning. It seemed like this must not be real. It seemed like I was watching from afar.

But it was real. Susan had died. My wife of forty years had died. And our family would never be the same again.

Susan and me

Most of us fear death—at least to some degree or in some way. Woody Allen said, "It is not that I fear death. I just don't want to be there when it happens." We may fear the fact that we will cease to exist. We may be afraid of the pain and suffering related to death. We may be afraid that there will be unfinished work or that we will not achieve our "purpose for living" before we die. Yet for all of us, our life's journey will end in death. We are all going to die. Living in denial of that fact does not change the reality that each of us will perish.

Most of us don't know when we will die, and none of us can be certain to even see tomorrow. When we face and then embrace the difficult fact that we, too, will die, we are set free. By facing this reality without fear, we are able to see the world in a new and fresh way. We are able to distinguish what is important from what is unimportant. We realize that everything we do for ourselves is temporary and will die with us. None of our possessions will matter much when we are gone. We realize that much of what we do for others is permanent and will live on in them and in their descendants. Many of the people we consider great teachers and spiritual leaders have come to this understanding. It is not easy, but by looking on our own death with love, we can love everything and everyone more. Confucius said, "If we don't know life, how can we know death?" I would add, "If we don't love death, how can we love life?"

Susan was an amazing teacher. She taught swimming to hundreds of people of all ages. She taught her children how to live life. She taught us to enjoy every day loving others. And she taught all of us how to die. She taught us that to fully live, we should not fear death. Instead, we should embrace it as part of life.

Susan also was a devout Christian. She taught us that we should have a purpose in our life. She taught us that we should put God first. She taught us that when we love God with all our heart, good things will happen both in our lives and afterward.

# The 2010s:
## It's All About Love

"Love is life. And if you miss love, you miss life."

*—Leo Buscaglia*

# CHAPTER FIFTEEN: THE FUZZY AFTERMATH

For me, the 2010s thus far have consisted of some positive changes super-imposed on negative global sameness. During this decade, the world drifted along in a haphazard and rudderless way, but signs of hope and revision also appeared. Examples of continued negative tedium in the world include: the never-ending Iraq War; the eurozone debt crisis; the protracted Arab-Israeli conflict; the new Cold War between the United States and Russia; the Mexican drug war; coups d'état in a number of countries; continued terrorist attacks; cyber hacking incidents; assassinations; targeted killings; and continued US economic malaise and global warming. Examples of positive change during this decade include: breakthroughs in science and technology; gains in the global treatment of many diseases; the rise of the "best-behaved youth" in America in decades; US urban renewal and revitalization; and the accelerated use of mobile phones to network and reinforce real-life global relationships.

My life has followed a similar course to my perception of global events because at first I was depressed and caught up in various stages of the grief cycle. Later I was able to see the good that had been all around me always. Gradually I was able to appreciate the good more and more. Finally a new love transformed my life to one of joy and contentment.

After Susan's death a large number of decisions had to be made. I made them all in a numb fog. My mind was not yet ready to fully face what had happened. We had the burial service just a few days later. It was a beautiful service highlighted by the release of doves at the end. In most burial ceremonies, the doves fly around in a circle and the white dove (symbolizing the deceased) joins the group. After completing several large circles, all the doves return to the dove keepers. The doves in Susan's ceremony behaved differently. Susan's white dove flew up with the others and became the lead dove in the flight. After completing one circle, the entire flock of doves flew up and out of sight forever. It was if Susan was showing all the other doves and all of us the way—to heaven.

There were numerous tasks to plan and orchestrate related to the burial service and the memorial service. There were pictures that had to be found and sorted. There was a need to find a location, find a person to officiate the service, plan the service, plan the program, contact performers, plan flowers for the coffin and for the service, and plan my own remarks to be presented at the service. I had help from family members for many of these tasks, but I felt responsible to Susan to make the services as nice as possible. During the memorial service, I wanted to circulate and visit at least briefly with all those who traveled to attend. When the service ended and all the friends left, I was exhausted.

While Susan was alive, all our friends and family made frequent visits to our home. We averaged about four to six visitors per day during the final five months from May through late September. We also had a minimum of four caregivers working in our home every day plus hospice nurses, bathers, and social workers. It was a crowded, almost carnivalesque atmosphere that required considerable accommodation from Roman and Tia, as well as me. Each day I was required to be friendly, personable, and willing to manage a troop of people. I was exhausted just managing the household.

Following Susan's death, my pain and my family's pain continued for several years. It was as if all of us were drifting without a rudder to steer us. My grief caused me to be somewhat disconnected from my family, friends, and the world. It took me several years to progress through my grief. I did not reach out to my friends and my friends did not reach out to me. All of my geology friends retreated. All of our former couple friends kept their distance. Instead of hosting eight or more adults per day, we now had no visitors at all for weeks at a time. Nobody called me on the telephone and I didn't call them. There was almost no contact with friends at all. Rob and Alisha and the grandkids moved nearby and that was a big help. Still, they were busy with their lives and I felt a little out of place when I was around them. Roman and Tia were still not adults and I had no adults in the house with whom I could discuss my day and share my deepest thoughts. In fact, I had never lived alone in my life. I went from living at home in high school to living in a fraternity in college. Then I was married for forty years. This new life, with no other adults present, was much more difficult than I expected. For the first time in my life, I was truly alone—and I felt lonely.

During the years after Susan's death, I told my family and friends that I was fine and that everything was going okay. I was in denial. In truth I knew that I frequently became angry for no apparent reason. Twice I had exploded in fits of rage in public, something I never would have done before Susan's death. I began going to counselors weekly to help with my grief processing and to cope with the difficulties of raising two special needs children alone. The counselors slowly helped me reconnect with the old me.

Roman had more difficulty identifying his feelings after the loss of his mother, but he was certainly impacted. He became angry and depressed at first and later more serious about life. He decided to make his own life more meaningful as a tribute to his mother.

Tia was impacted greatly by her mother's death and I felt great sorrow for her. She had been praying to God every night that her mother might live. When Susan died, she was clearly devastated. Tia shed many tears during both days and nights during the next few weeks after Susan's death. Life continued to be difficult for Tia, but the support and friendship she received from Alisha and Rob helped considerably. And during the next several years, her therapist, Dr. H., worked wonders with Tia and helped her through her grieving process.

When I finally progressed through all the stages of my grief, I was able to change my attitude. Gradually I began to view the world as a good place again. Eventually I began to view other people as innocent and loveable. My life and my family's lives started to improve. Through hard work, Roman began to progress in school and in his social life. Rob and Alisha helped Tia adjust first to junior high and then to high school. Roman worked very hard to return to public school and to succeed there. Tia completed driver's education and became an excellent driver. I was able to begin to enjoy all aspects of my life again, so I decided to join a dating website for single people over fifty. Predictably, my life was about to really change for the better.

# CHAPTER SIXTEEN: LOVE ANEW

I was a participant on the dating website for less than a week when I noticed a very beautiful and wonderful woman named Carol. Carol and I corresponded for a few days before arranging a coffee date in downtown Boise. For both of us, it was "like at first sight." Love would come later, but not much later.

Carol was amazing, bright, and articulate. She had worked as a counselor for long-term caregivers. She was a loving and caring woman who had lost her husband to cancer. She had no children, but she didn't mind taking on that responsibility. An Idaho native, she had lived in Boise a long time. She was beautiful on the inside as well as on the outside—perfect in every way.

Carol and I began a dating relationship in July 2013, which led to a fully-fledged romantic relationship. Soon we were spending more and more time together, dining together or attending movies. We spent time at each other's homes. Our love for each other was growing day by day. It was glorious to be in love again with a one-of-a-kind woman. Every day took on new meaning from the moment I awoke. It was magnificent to be alive and in love!

During Roman's birthday celebration in late August, Carol met Roman, Tia, Rob, Alisha, and my grandchildren. We floated the Boise River together in a rented raft. Carol liked my family and they loved her! In early September, Carol had hip replacement surgery. I did my best to support her during and after the surgery. I met Carol's mother and sister because they had traveled to Boise from southern Utah to help her, as well. Carol's mother was very sweet and gentle. She reminded me a good deal of my own mother. Carol's sister, Connie, was a true gem. She had raised a lovely family and was an exemplary wife, mother, and grandmother. We both liked each other. Carol went through the surgery with flying colors and she was up and walking later that same day. She recovered well during the next few months.

In the early fall, we traveled together to Phoenix, Arizona, where we experienced the aerial thrill of a hot air balloon ride and a rousing concert by an aging but still spry Jimmy Buffett. When we returned to Boise, our closeness grew. We had many deep and intimate conversations and learned as much as we could about each other. In the late fall, we traveled together to Costa Rica, where we lived in a hut in the forest canopy at Lapa Rios Eco Lodge. The sights, smells, and sounds of the jungle both day and night were thrilling.

In December, we stayed in Boise for Christmas. Both Tia and Roman wanted to spend a Christmas here because we had traveled so much during Christmastime in the past. After the holiday, Carol, Roman, and I traveled to McCall, Idaho, for wintertime fun on snowshoes and skates. We rented a nice cabin, where we luxuriated in the hot tub surrounded by crisp white snow.

On the morning of the first day of 2014, I got down on one knee before Carol and asked her to marry me. She whispered yes, and my heart soared. We would now start planning our marriage and our life together. We told Roman right away and then we told Tia and Alisha and Kim when we returned to Boise. Everyone in my family was very happy because they loved Carol.

In the springtime, Carol and I traveled to Sequim, Washington, to do some repairs and clean out some of our accumulated junk at our house there. We also made a quick trip to Victoria, BC. Carol was moved by the beauty at our Sequim home and I was reminded how much I enjoy that part of the world.

The wedding of Patrick and Carol on April 19, 2014.

Finally, the day came: on April 19, 2014, Carol and I were united as one in marriage. The ceremony was held in the courtyard at Berryhill and Co. Restaurant. John Berryhill was Carol's friend, and he made sure that the setting and food were perfect. The sunny day helped brighten our immense love for each other and for our family and friends. Michelle Tae, Carol's friend, officiated the wedding and made the ceremony very special by helping us to be fully present in the moment. She reminded us of the sights, smells, and sounds that would help us to remember this time and our love always. Roman bravely offered a toast to our happiness, and he welcomed Carol into the family. Both of us were greatly in love on that day—and have been every day since.

Cavanaugh family at wedding of Patrick and Carol. Charles, Ken, Alisha Palmer, Kya Palmer, Tia, Huxly Palmer, Patrick, Carol, Roman, Shydyn Palmer, Betty Hill, and Rob Palmer.

We moved our two households into a beautiful thirty-year-old home on Table Rock Road. In June, we held a wedding reception for all of our friends in the backyard. It was deeply moving to visit (however briefly) with all the people near and far who love us and support us.

Our honeymoon consisted of a Peruvian trip to Cusco, Machu Picchu, and Lake Titicaca. We stayed in Palacio del Inka in Cusco, a five-star hotel built on the foundation of an Incan palace. The Incan stonework in the bar is phenomenal. In the Sacred Valley, we stayed at Sonesta Posadas del Inca Yucay, which is housed in a renovated former colonial-style monastery in the Sacred Valley, halfway between Cusco and Macchu Picchu. During the trip, Carol and I were able to get away and reflect on many different Incan ruins, and together we learned much about the culture. We also really enjoyed meeting and visiting with the Uros people who live on the reed islands in Lake Titicaca. The Uros use bundles of dried totora reeds to make reed boats and even to construct the islands themselves.

Together Carol and I have also traveled to Hawaii and to France. We stayed on the Big Island in Hawaii and rediscovered the island together. In France we traveled on two different river cruises, north from Paris on the Seine and south on the Rhone and Saone rivers. We loved Paris, the Palace of Versailles, Monet's Garden, the Cathedral at Rouen, the city of Lyon, and the bridge at Avignon. We noticed a tremendous police and military presence in Paris just three weeks before all the terrorist attacks. We will never forget our ride on an old steam-engine train in Tournon-Viviers.

Carol has been a wonderful addition to my life, and to Roman and Tia's lives. Through her kindness and devotion, she has brought many special abilities into our family: spirituality, organization, persistence, wisdom, and love. In fact, Carol is one of the most spiritual people I know. She believes that there is a spiritual connection to all things in the universe. She helps me to look for God in all people and to be receptive to things we don't understand.

Carol and Patrick in Zion National Park

At the same time, Carol is very grounded and pragmatic, and I have come to admire her organization and efficiency. Each day she exercises, meditates, and plans. At the end of each day, she reflects on what has happened and journals her feelings. She keeps an organized calendar and makes sure that none of us misses any appointments.

Carol doesn't shy away from life's challenges, empowered by the knowledge that if she persists, she will accomplish her goals. And Carol is so very wise. She knows the things that are important and the things that are trivial. She helps me to stay on task and focus on the meaningful things in my life.

Finally, Carol is a very loving woman, radiating with love for me and Roman and Tia. She also has much love in her heart for Kim, Alisha, and other members of our family. And she adores and values all of her friends—just as they are. Carol has helped me recover from the loss of my mother in 2012 and aided my father in getting the treatment he needed when he broke his back in 2013. Finally, she has given me great comfort following the accidental death of my sister, Mary, in 2013.

Fortunately, Tia has recently started to progress in her life. She has developed a more loving and positive attitude and has begun to emerge as a young woman. She excels in practical knowledge and common sense abilities. Both Carol and I think her future is very bright.

During the summer of 2014, Tia traveled with a People to People student group to England, Ireland, Scotland, and Wales. She seemed to enjoy the travel, the adventure, and especially the companionship of the other students. During the summer of 2016, Tia traveled with her sisters Kim and Alisha to Mozambique. They all were part of a group that experienced the restoration of Gorongosa National Park by an international team. It was an excellent experience for Tia and hopefully will spur her interest in becoming a biologist or wildlife photographer.

Eventually Roman recognized that he would be better off with a fresh start and some hard work. This year, Roman graduated from Boise High and he will attend Boise State University this fall. Roman's mother would be very proud of his daily efforts and academic progress thus far. Roman has really turned the corner and begun to emerge as an energetic young gentleman.

According to Abraham Maslow's hierarchy of needs, once our basic needs for food, shelter, and safety are satisfied, our next greatest need is for love and belongingness. Psychologists agree that it is part of our essence to love and to be loved. Humans need love to live completely. Many of us think about love and our loved ones much of the day. We humans all talk about love. Most of our songs are about love. We all know something about love. But do we really *know* love? Do we really know what it means to love? There are many different kinds of love and we use the word *love* to signify many things. We might say we "love" hamburgers or apple pie. Frequently, when we talk about love, we are not talking about real love. We sometimes might even say "I love you" to people whom we don't really love.

My mother taught me that for real love to exist, it requires three critical responsibilities. The first responsibility is that real love has no conditions. When we truly love someone, our love doesn't stop regardless of what they do or say. The second responsibility is that real love is selfless. Real love doesn't want or need anything in return. The final responsibility of real love is that it is complete acceptance of the other person. Real love allows the other to be exactly as they are with no changes required. Real love has the power to heal and transform any situation and bring deep meaning to our lives. Real love conquers all.

In order to really love, we have to first learn how to love ourselves and accept ourselves with all our warts and imperfections. Then we can offer loving-kindness to others. We must also be able to understand our own suffering in order to bring true compassion to others. If we have joy in our hearts, we can offer our joy to others. Real love depends on our ability to understand how we are all connected. We all share many things in this universe, and what touches one of us touches us all.

Our natural fulfillment comes from loving others. Our love is organic and it must continue to grow and be applied to more and more people or it will wither and die. We have the natural capacity to learn to love everyone we encounter. We don't have to limit the number of people whom we love. Feelings of happiness, joy, and completion come from giving real love away freely and without fear or judgment.

Carol has taught me many lessons, many of which are summarized in one of her favorite books, *Love Is Letting Go of Fear* by Dr. Gerald Jampolsky. In the book, Dr. Jampolsky takes many of his ideas from an earlier book series, *A Course in Miracles*. The central thread of these books is the notion that we can achieve self-fulfillment through love giving. The author suggests that we first make peace of mind our primary goal and that we let go of our preoccupation with the past and the future. Then we are able to forgive others and to see everyone as guiltless. By seeing others as guiltless, we can let go of fear by living in the now rather than in the past or future. Along the way, we learn to accept direction from our inner intuitive voices. By realizing that each of us is completely filled with love all the time and that we have plenty to give away to everyone, we are able to give our love unconditionally with no expectation of a return.

Carol has taught me to be involved in a process of personal transformation in which I am concerned about giving. She has awakened the knowledge in me that the essence of my being is love and that my life should be about loving others.

# CHAPTER SEVENTEEN: SOME FINAL THOUGHTS

In some ways this story of my life is the Pollyanna version. I have chosen to omit many of life's problems and struggles. Perhaps that is a disservice to my readers, but I hope not. I do think that almost all of my readers know that those challenges come to us all. Sometimes the challenges *seem* so great that it is difficult to continue moving forward. But the challenges of life are just a part of what our Divine Creator gives us. He also gives us the joys, the gifts, and the benefits of love. I would rather focus on the positives than the negatives.

Each of the seven lessons that I learned in seven decades of living is still very relevant today. Today some of our freedom in America has been lost. Most of us no longer can leave our homes or our cars unlocked. We are concerned for our children's safety when they are not at home. We can no longer board airplanes as quickly and as easily as we did in the past. Now we must have complex sets of passwords to protect our identity. Our fears of evil people have limited our freedoms. Some political candidates and television news programs are making us even more fearful of certain groups. Just as we were once afraid of communists, today some people would have us fear Muslims. One of my best friends is a Muslim man from Egypt. Tito is a great friend and a loving family man. He is a great example of a hardworking American. Because I don't fear Muslims, I have the freedom to experience a fuller life with friends like Tito.

Certainly our friendships are just as valuable today as they were in the 1960s. For me, friends still provide a sounding board for my ideas. They make sports more enjoyable. They also support me and help pick me up when I am down. They still make my joy more complete.

My family continues to be central to my life. I deeply regret losing the most loving human I have ever known, my mother. I also deeply regret losing my dear sister, Mary. It is wonderful having my brother, Ken, now living in Boise. My oldest daughters are grown and have lives of their own, but they both still are very close and both provide support and love. My younger children are in the process of leaving the nest and experiencing life on their own. My grandchildren, fortunately, live only five miles away and I smile when I see them. We have family dinners every week to keep our family bonds strong.

The search for gold was not a shortcut to wealth. I earned my good fortune by working very hard over a long time period. I am proud of my career and I am proud to have worked with so many wonderful geologists. Many of them remain my friends today. I am proud that more than one thousand men and women work at the South Pipeline Mine and soon they will be mining the Crossroads deposit on claims still owned by ECM, Inc. To stay connected with my profession, I now collect meteorites, gold samples, and fossils. My Mars meteorite collection is one of the world's finest, but my greatest joy is giving school presentations on geologic topics.

I am so thankful that Susan and I left our comfort zone. I am very happy we hosted exchange students, and I learned a great deal from them. I thank God for having Roman and Tia in our lives every day. They both warm my heart and add greatly to our family. My life would be very different if we had not made the choice to adopt and if we had not had the courage to follow through in Roman and Tia's lives.

I still miss Susan and think about her always. Because Susan lived her faith, I know that she is with God in Heaven. I pray that some day I will be with her. I know that if I love God and my neighbors, God will reward my faithfulness. And only a few of us know how much time we have left on this planet. It helps to realize we must make the most of every day. We must live for others and live for now. Knowing we will all die frees me up from worrying about the past or the future. Now is my time. Now is perhaps all I have.

I am blessed with much love in my life. For me, God is love. I hope that all people find ways to send love into the world. Leo Buscaglia was one of the strongest influences on Susan and me in the 1980s and 1990s. We both loved his books, and our "love circle" group in Billings discussed many of his ideas for months on end. In addition to his focus on loving relationships, Leo believed that we all have complete responsibility for the way we perceive the world. He believed that through love, all of us have the power to change our own lives and our outcomes.

This world is not always fair. But it is true that we all get back pretty much what we give. It is as if the world is an echo returning our love. This is one of Leo's many famous quotes, and I think it is a good final thought: "Don't spend your precious time asking why the world isn't a better place. It will only be time wasted. The question to ask is: How can *I* make it better? To that, there is an answer."

CPSIA information can be obtained
at www.ICGtesting.com
Printed in the USA
LVOW05*2045121116
512167LV00001B/1/P

9 781635 050677